too hurt to love

cynthia a. cook

Foreword by Ben Carson

REVIEW AND HERALD® PUBLISHING ASSOCIATION
HAGERSTOWN, MD 21740

The author assumes full responsibility for the accuracy of
all facts and quotations as cited in this book.

This book was
Edited by Jeannette R. Johnson
Designed by Patricia S. Wegh
Cover photo by Joel D. Springer
Interior photo by PhotoDisc
Typeset: 12/14 Garamond Light

PRINTED IN U.S.A.

02 01 00 99 98   5 4 3 2 1

R&H Cataloging Service
Cook, Cynthia A.
    Too hurt to love.

    1. Child abuse. 2. Abused women. 3. Stepfamily.
I. Title.

            306.874

ISBN 0-8280-1293-8

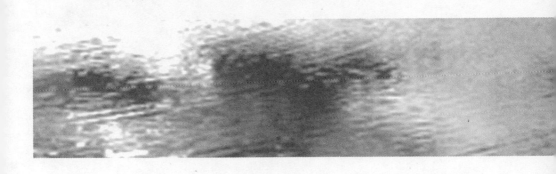

Dedication

To my incredible family,
who loved me through being too hurt to love.

To Hank, my husband, who was unwilling to let me go.

To Kell, my firstborn,
who has tried to make sense of the chaos she knew in me.

To Buff, my secondborn,
who let me know she couldn't.

To Doug, her husband,
who supported her in supporting me.

To Scott, my thirdborn,
who inspired me to heal my wounds and to love.

And, most of all, to God, that I have such a story to tell.

To order additional copies of *Too Hurt to Love,*
by Cindy Cook, call **1-800-765-6955.**

Visit us at www.rhpa.org for more information
on Review and Herald products.

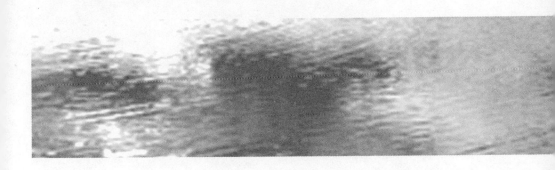

Acknowledgments

How do I begin to express the gratefulness I feel for every support received from friends and family? Along with childhood pain has come a matching dole of grace more gentle, more buoyant, and more encouraging than I can describe. Without Ben and Candy Carson's encouragement, I would never have begun this undertaking, and there would have never been a story written. Somehow they recognized in me what I could not see then. I am very grateful for such dear and visionary friends. Joe Wheeler, the first one to read my manuscript, bolstered my hopes and encouraged me on. Penny Wheeler invested her time and energy to refine my script. Richard Fredericks offered timely and valuable suggestions. I have been blessed by Jeannette Johnson, my editor, who has so patiently shared her sensitive efforts in guiding and chiseling this love story to its presentation. To my husband and children I owe my deepest appreciation for their ability to join me, to confront me, to love me.

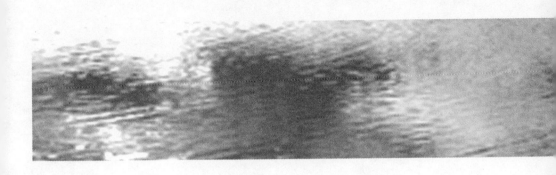

Contents

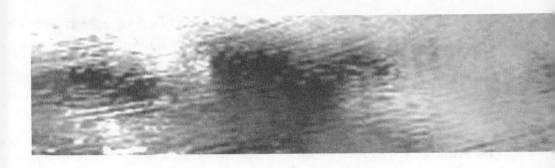

Preface

No one's story is all one's own. Unique, yes, but not of one's own creation, nor of one's own keeping. So I share my story with you. The risk of vulnerability is one I must take so that you may know the hope of impossible things.

This is a story of how perceptions developed from infancy on can derail the ability to love one's self and, therefore, inhibit the ability to love others. It portrays the chronic effects a fractured childhood can produce, the aftermath itself spawning its own escalation of shame and confusion. It portrays what this cost me—and my family. But it is also the story of how unconditional love *can* change a heart and heal a past. It's the story of healing an unrelenting hemorrhage of the heart.

It never needs to take so long to change these feelings; it never needs to cost this terrible price. It happens the instant you understand how God loves you. You, in this very moment. You, with no changes made at all. You, *exactly* the way you are now. Despite everything.

But this knowing of His love is sometimes so hard to come by. We are too hurt to love, too hurt to know it. Sometimes He must use the most unlikely, the most unexpected, means to penetrate early beliefs about ourselves, those terrible core beliefs, often set up at birth. Those beliefs that tell us, "I am worthless," "My experience is not true," and, "I don't matter." Although God's giving of His Son proves our unspeakable value, some of us can't believe it. And penetrating this misbelief is the greatest miracle of all (Gen. 3:15).

There is no heart that cannot be healed when the right chord is touched. He knows our intimacies. He knows our most hidden secrets. He knows our deepest hurts, our greatest fears. And He knows how to reach us.

Your way may not be my way. But know there is a way for you. Be willing. Watch for His touch. God will find a way to reach you, to let you know His love unconditionally. When you do, I promise you, you will be able to love yourself. You will love even those who seem to you to be the most unlovable of all.

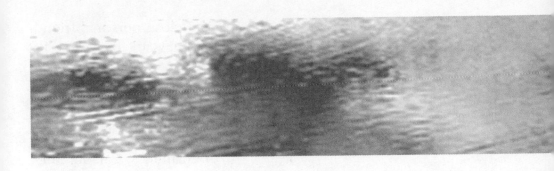

Foreword

Many people who call themselves Christians do not know the joy of life in Christ. Through the masterful use of metaphors and imagery, Cindy Cook tells a story that in some sense is common to millions of wounded Christians. At times the reader will ask, "How can anyone be so confused as this woman was?" Yet careful introspection will reveal that her experiences of confusion and pain are common to most Christians who have not yet discovered what the love of God really does in a person's life.

One of Satan's most effective tricks is to make us feel that we cannot love ourselves, that we are unworthy, that we are worms to be squashed underfoot. This book provides a step-by-step journey from that feeling of worthlessness to the overwhelming joy of knowing that the Owner and Creator of the entire universe has so much love for each one of us that He willingly made the supreme sacrifice to save our souls. He has already paid the price, and we cause Him great suffering by not accepting Him.

The ultimate benefit of Cindy's story is for those millions of Christians who have not experienced the joy of God's salvation, and who feel that they have something to do with their own salvation, when in fact Jesus has paid it all. It is an exceptional thing to be able to put into words the feelings that are so common and destructive—and so elusive. Cindy Cook has done us all a great service by articulating these feelings, offering solutions through

God and His love. I am proud that she is a close personal friend; I have benefited tremendously through the years from her insights. I hope that you too will experience her sensitivity and wisdom, as well as her pain that was transformed into joy, through an appropriate journey with a God who is always there, though not always appreciated.

Benjamin S. Carson, M.D.

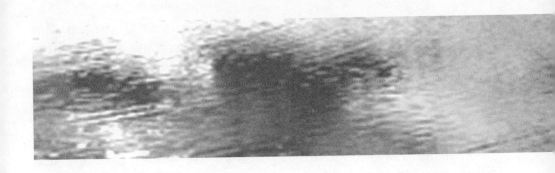

Introduction

My childhood events were a mélange of subtle offenses that inadvertently occurred between times so good that even Norman Rockwell would have admired them. The good times, like the bad times, evolved from our extended family interaction. More than 15 people inhabited Nana and Grampa's large Victorian home on a thriving chicken farm, situated at the gateway to Cape Cod.

The house was lovely, even in those days. A screened-in, sit-down porch skirted the garden side of the house, where hedges teemed with blooms of vibrant color that overwhelmed the senses. There were 13 rooms in all, each upstairs bedroom claimed by my father's brothers and their families and by Nana and Grampa. Memory is rich with sounds of creaking floors, the aroma of molasses cookies mingled with burning wood, and low-hung ceilings a child could lie in bed and push her feet up against. Wallpapered yellow cabbage roses with interwoven vines covered the dining room walls, and wild mini-bouquets of buttercups in pint jelly glasses brightened the enamel kitchen table.

We were pillars in a New England community surviving the end of World War II. From the outside looking in, we were a nice family, well respected in town. Nana attended the Congregational Church in the center, baked for bazaars, and brought flowers to the sick. The bustle of activity within our large household could accommodate anyone without a lot of deliberation. My uncles and grandfather mostly worked at chicken farming; Nana and my aunts mostly "familied." My father was an eighth-generation Yankee; my mother the daughter of a poor Italian immigrant family. They married in July 1942 and took up their dwelling at my grandparents' home. It was almost three years before my parents conceived a child. Eighteen hours of hard labor left my mom exhausted.

And she was certainly unprepared for the sudden care of a sick baby. Nevertheless, within two weeks I was hospitalized with pneumonia—before penicillin. They weren't sure I would survive this illness. The crisis continued for three precarious weeks, balancing me between life and death, while Mom and Dad watched with a concern that knotted their lives together. Gradually, as I began to improve, their spirits lifted, and I was brought home where we settled into our corner of the house to establish ourselves as a family within a family.

Concerns over my health flowed between my parents; they hovered and worried, then faced further distress when I was 2 and hospitalized for a second bout of pneumonia. Resulting anxieties and tensions affected my emerging perspective, and I attempted to express myself through tantrums that eventually baffled the entire household. Holding my breath and fainting was more than they could handle, so my parents called the doctor to inquire how to handle this child who had survived two crises, yet was now creating another. He told them what to do: "Place her in the middle of the bathroom floor, walk out, and close the door behind you."

They followed his directions explicitly. I cried until I could no longer breathe. Then I stopped. The silence must have seemed eternal as they waited behind the closed door. At last, I screamed again, rallying to life on their terms. They were delighted that I never had a temper tantrum again, but that was the day I finally understood a tragic lesson: Expressing certain emotions meant abandonment. Unfortunately, it was customary then to thwart a child's behaviors at all costs, and my parents knew no other resources for sorting out their dilemma. In the end, no one understood what I didn't have words to say.

Tickling sounds so innocent, but I had an uncle who teased

mercilessly, if not by a derrogatory comment, then by his incessant tickling that wore me out. It went beyond fun to something else. Adult sport turned into my nightmare—and left its mark.

I never knew when he would decide he needed a good laugh, so I recoiled whenever he walked toward me. I can still see his flannel shirt and smell the acrid scent of chicken feathers and grain. Hay from board floors where chicken manure accumulated stuck to his brown boots. His hair, hat-rumpled; a disheveled look in his eyes.

Without warning, he would bend over, swallowing me up, relentless hands moving in for the kill. I would wait in my mind for it to stop. A strange kind of waiting. A razor-edge waiting.

"Stop, stop!" I would hear my voice grow fainter and fainter until no sound at all came out. Forced laughter became silent screams, floating out to nowhere. I wouldn't be able to breathe, crumpled on the floor, curled in my dilemma against the mopboard. Finally, for no conceivable reason, the tickling would end. Breathing came back slowly. I would eventually uncurl and furtively scurry away to lick my wounds. I can still remember his responses. When at last I would come to, belittling my pain, he would assure me that what I had experienced had not really happened.

"Oh, come on; it's nothing. It can't be *that* bad!" Or, more snidely, "*I* don't feel a thing, so *you* have nothing to cry about!"

Lest I lead you to believe it was all bad, I must relate our "good times," too. Christmases were scenes to register on the joyful side of things: aproned moms bending over the oven; back-slapping men lifting eggnog high, toasting; and children enthralled with the reality of Santa. We left cookies. We wrote notes. We watched and waited. We knew he lived. No one could have convinced us otherwise. In summer we embellished our doll carriages with crepe paper and ribbons to qualify for doll carriage parades. On other days we lay on the grass and counted how long it took clouds to blow out of sight, held buttercups beneath our chins to find the "butter secret," or did cartwheels (when the grass was dry enough). My cousins and I, we compared all we knew of life.

Ordinary interaction, normal responses, common scoldings— they were not mean, for my parents did what they thought was right. However, even "nice" families may unintentionally hurt their children. And when, from the child's perspective, too many subtle abuses stack up higher than the child, there is often a hidden yet grievous aftermath. Thus the negative messages drilled into me seemed to pile up, amassing, I suspect, a greater influence than was intended. Having no frame of reference, no scale of relative value, I took it all to heart.

Like many other children, I collected subtleties. But subtleties confuse children. When everything else appears normal, children often conclude that "they" must be the problem. Sometimes adults validate that conclusion by voicing it within the child's hearing. This is especially damaging, since children take in such messages and responses and base their self-worth upon this feedback from those they trust the most. Hence, these negative reinforcements from adult authority figures tend to become self-fulfilling prophecies.

One afternoon I overheard my grandmother and uncle discussing my behavior. Standing eye-level to Nana's silver teapot, I saw the reflection of a 4-year-old girl who was being vividly described.

"That one! She *is* a brat! I don't know why they don't deal with her. *I* would, if I had my way. Mark my word, she is just terrible!"

It was agonizingly clear. I had been a failure from the beginning—and now they wished I were gone! As an only child, I assumed that I was so bad that my parents didn't want any more children. Yet I felt I had to be awfully good, since I was all they had. It was an impossible paradox.

The tragedy is not so much that they thought this of me, but that I bought into their opinion and turned against myself. It was a very simple yet profound decision that affected the majority of my life: I decided not to be me. If I was to make it in this family— or in this world—I had to be whomever they wanted me to be. To me, they were bigger, stronger, nicer, wiser. And, after all, my life depended on them. Nothing *could* be their fault. It had to be mine. So I believed their perception of me. Unfortunately, I was unable to distinguish what was real, or who I really was, and became hypervigilant to protect the facade I had invented until I lost track of my own person altogether. I didn't sense the pain of this decision until years later, after it had festered for a very long time.

too hurt to love

chapter 1

The Woodpile

I don't know why I thought it would be easier than it was. Seven years ago I would have never dreamed I could be filled with this kind of hatred. I had a loving husband, two precious daughters . . . and a son. With no threatening losses in our future, my life should have been peaceful, secure—even harmonious. Instead, whether I was folding laundry, carrying groceries in from the car, or just peeling potatoes for our dinner, I felt like a death-row prisoner facing execution.

Often change is spurred by hitting bottom—bottom being our own personal hell at its worst. This was mine.

≈

It is a crystal-clear Sunday morning in early October 1988 when I realize I am losing my mind. We're outside early, before 9:00, already sorting logs from the crude pile in our backyard. Tossing the heavy ones to the right, the smaller ones to the left, arranging them around the splitter for sizing down to fit the woodstove. Usually this exercise invigorates me, seems worth the effort. But not today. Today I know something is going awry.

I keep stumbling and tripping, my feet feel clumsy, catching on jagged logs. Using every muscle, I yank stuck pieces of wood loose, one by one, heaving them with all my might to the sawdust-covered ground beside the splitter.

too hurt to love

The old wordless rage rises from the pit of my stomach. I feel it swelling inside, choking me. It's worse than ever. In a fleeting second I wonder how I can feel this violent inside when the sky is so blue and the air so crisp outside. But there is no stopping it, this rage that refuses to be whipped into line. With a fierceness it persists now, without a break.

At the edge of sanity, I feel my mind begin to shatter under the fury, to break down altogether. One thought persistently hammers through my head, a senseless thought that keeps getting louder and louder: *If only I could kill something . . . someone. Destroy life—like mine has been destroyed.* This seemed to be my only out, my single hope that might lessen this intolerable pressure.

I work mechanically—bend, grab, lift, toss. One log after another. My hands work, but my mind drifts, then jolts into a flashback.

Suddenly I see the woman again. I am in the car, hurtling toward her as she pauses for a moment, then steps off the curb into the street. Oblivious to me, she marches straight ahead, and I *stomp* the gas pedal, clutch the steering wheel, and roar on! I know she'll keep coming. Know instinctively she doesn't see me. Know we'll connect. But *I don't care!* I *want* to hit her! Oh, God, I *want* to *kill* her!

I wait. No sound; no bump. I know I've missed her—and feel outraged. Killing that woman would have been a relief!

As I stand here, trying to balance on one huge log that juts out from the rest, I know I am not safe. I flee the woodpile, sweat coursing down my back, feeling my head nearly separating from my body as I run across the wet grass to the house. Evergreens blur to fuzziness; the gravel drive seems to rise up waist-high. Loose leaves collect on the heels of my shoes, but there's no wiping them off now. Everything is wrong; I'm desperate. I need to call Sue, my friend from the 12-step meetings. Sue will help me.

"Sue, I'm so angry!" I erupt into the phone. Then, stammering, I continue. "I just—I want—I have to kill someone."

She's obligated to rebuke me, but she doesn't. Instead, she speaks calmly into the receiver. "Tell me about it, honey."

The support I hear in her voice tears me apart. I can't swallow the sobs anymore. "I just can't stand this any longer," I hear myself choking into the phone. "I'm afraid . . . I'm so angry . . . I can't manage it. I need help. I need this thing gone! Is there someplace I could go to have emotional surgery?"

"Yes, honey, there sure is! You can go to a treatment center in Pennsylvania. I have many friends who've gotten help there." She sounds incredibly hopeful, even as I'm dying.

I call the center that bright October Sunday, not knowing if I'll live to see 1989.

The registrar tells me the first opening is in March. My heart sinks. March is too late! I appeal for an earlier admission, and she promises to call if a cancellation occurs, but I phone weekly, begging them to check again.

Finally, the week before Christmas, a cancellation calls in! Over the phone, I give my name, address, phone number, and credit card number. No, no insurance. I'll use my savings. This is my "rainy day," my very rainy day.

Stress often ambushes me via back pain, and by now it's acute. I lay on our living room floor most of that weekend, staring at the ceiling, my feet raised to rest on the brick hearth. To escape the commotion erupting around him, my husband, Hank, has taken Scott, his son, to visit his sisters in Tennessee for the week. My daughter, Buff, is sure I ought to go nowhere in this condition. I assure her I have no choice. Everything is falling apart. Desperation overrules family objections and common sense. I *am* going.

The family is keenly aware of my obvious estrangement from Scott. Family gatherings are polluted by it. More than anything, they wish it would dissolve, wish I could be a mother to him. Not a stepmother. Not any part of estranged. A warm, loving, full-fledged mother to him. But that is impossible!

Wrestling my bag into the car, I make a careful adjustment to the car seat, scrunching my spine into position, and head north. Rain is liquid gray against the car windows; I focus my eyes on the taillights ahead of me. I have to get to this place. My chances, clanging loosely behind me, are about to fall off.

Immense gray fieldstones shape the large Victorian mansion. A white-railed porch runs full across the front. Towering evergreens nestle tightly against the north side, and walking trails flow out from every side like ribbons on a Maypole. But there is no dancing now. Under the green porch roof, rocking chairs tip to a moist breeze. Other travel bags wait in place by the steps. All seems quiet. I step into a hallway, looking for someone to direct me, but no one is here. I'm early. Registration begins at 4:00; it's only 3:30.

I feel like a stick of dynamite that's one spark away from explosion. The quiet hallway echoes with my heartbeat. Panic turns sour in my throat. *Where are they? Why aren't they here early? Surely I'm not the first person to come 30 minutes ahead of time!*

My fears flare before me. *Is this all a hoax? Will I leave no different than when I arrived?* The gray tar horizon still stretches endlessly ahead, slow and dull, without a future, without hope. Completely weary, I sink against a wall. Books, sermons, friends, counseling, praying. I have tried them all, but nothing has offered the strength to flip my world around. Miracles, like fairy tales, just happen to elusive characters, manipulated into existence through a clever imagination. There is nothing concrete about them at all.

In that last moment before someone arrives to begin the admissions process, I'm forced to reflect back on my life.

I am 43 years old. Though I've professed Christianity all my life, I carry a hatred I can barely stifle, that bursts out of me irrationally, crazily, in unspeakable ways, toward my stepson. How I hate to be in the house when he's there! To pick up the little Kleenex balls he tosses—and misses—toward the wastebasket! To use anything he's touched! To sit beside him at the table! How I bristle when he speaks! How I avoid hanging his clothes next to mine on the clothesline! I spend my day obsessed with trying to get as far away from him as I can. I'm horrified by the intensity of my resentment. I'm confused by it, ashamed of it. Something is terribly wrong.

I'm miserable. And I'm enraged that I should be so stuck. I feel beyond hope. Beyond tears. I truly want to die. But a tiny voice somewhere deep inside me begs me to keep going, to be absolutely sure there isn't the slightest chance of a miracle. I have to know.

What *has* happened to me? How did I get here? Oh, how I wish it were all just some terrible nightmare that would disappear in the opening of an eyelid.

too hurt to love

chapter 2

The Beginning

How did I ever get myself into this position? I'd been so reluctant to marry again. Yet here I am, trying to do a job I have never felt qualified to do, all based on a single promise—and on letting my heart trust it. Into this second marriage I have brought my children and all the proverbial baggage, merging the kinds of needs that only early losses can produce.

~

It's the summer of 1980. The religious community in New Hampshire, where we live, is filled with festivities for the weekend. Every year we celebrate with similar communities from various parts of New England, so this year we are all excited to see old friends again.

In New Hampshire the ground bursts into bloom for only a few months, and this is one of those days of burgeoning color. Beneath an arching cerulean sky, the wind carries mingled fragrances of roasted corn, freshly sliced onions, and fuchsia and white phlox dusted brilliant in the sunshine lying across their uplifted faces. Bronzed sticks of brittle grass stab mercilessly at our bare feet, but the girls and I lug huge steel basins of corn over to the boiling pots on the campfire stove.

Out of the corner of my eye I see Buff, my youngest daughter, slowing down. She stops midfield, puts down her pan, and picks a stuck blade from between her toes. She glances up at me and scrunches her face into a look that says she wishes she'd worn her rubber thongs. Kell and I nod in agreement, but persist under the added weight of corn, bracing the soles of our own feet against injury.

Buff is almost 12. She's finally thinned out from her baby plumpness (and lost her lisp) and wears a retainer at night to nudge her front teeth inward. Hair the color of ginger in the sunshine frames her full face, high-cheekboned and rosy. A barrette clipping her ponytail to the back of her head gives the strange appearance of feathers protruding from the back of her head. Wisps fly straight up and forward onto the roundedness of her forehead. She is dressed today in a mahogany cotton jumper, flecked with tangerine blossoms. Shoulder straps catch a bib front, covering a peach-colored T-shirt with smudges of soot already on the sleeves. Her almond eyes, matching the shape of her father's, fill with a twinkle all her own.

Buff has an affinity to people. She can sense an ache a mile away, and everything in her is devoted to making it better. She can sidle up to a person, old or young, and know how to unveil their heart for them. Most find her forthrightness refreshing; her innocence irresistible. Yet Buff is lonely. She carries an emptiness she can't understand. She wants her daddy's heart, but finds over and over again that it's unavailable in the way she needs it.

We hoist three basins of unhusked corn onto the steamy wood and ashes. Just enough heat to sweeten those succulent kernels, and just enough time for Buff to visit with friends before dinner. Kelly, my firstborn, and I walk toward the huge tent. Its green stripes curve over the top and down the sides, aligning with ropes yanked firmly against the stakes. Shade offers little relief, but we sit to examine the soles of our feet and wonder if it's worth a trip back to the house for thongs.

Kell, at 16, knows too much of the hard side of life. She can grow vegetables and bake bread. She's stood beside me and cooked a meal for 20 and served it graciously. From scratch, we whip together our own almond milk, or make Jack cheese from cashews, and we could write the book on 101 ways to serve applesauce or oatmeal. She excels scholastically and is beginning to feel like a misfit in the small, one-room school on our campus. Our whole family history is portrayed in her face. High cheekbones proclaim Indian heritage somewhere long ago in the Wampanoag tribe. Sprinkled freckles reveal the Irish, the Italian. Dark chestnut hair is flying loose from a single braid midway down her back. Already in the sun too long, her tan face and arms move expertly, smoothing her skirt of turquoise plaid across her lap, tucking in the white ruffled blouse that hangs halfway out. Fixing herself, she knows the party is about to begin. But the party will be a simple event. I sit beside her, grateful, yet not really grasping the magnificence of who she is. A quick look into my eyes, a half-smile mirroring between us, and without a word exchanged I know we are together in that time, at that place. Then she turns again to her 16-year-old musings.

Several ankle-length skirts swish against themselves across the burnt lawn, moving between the shaded areas and the beating sunshine. Men clad in overalls and dungarees shake hands and back-slap each other in greeting. Low murmurings among long-lost acquaintances, and the convention rolls on.

There must be 300 here. These spiritual feasts are known to rally souls hungry for something of substance. They seek the tough biblical truth, something they can bite into with all their strength, with a fury from some unsatisfied passion, all in the name of obedience. Yet I wonder if we aren't really seeking something to flip our unbalanced spheres back on kilter, where we might even steady ourselves and find a God worth celebrating.

It is on this day that I meet Hank.

chapter 3

His Proposal

The proposal sends me reeling backward. Remarriage! The mere thought of it appears like a phantom ghost, both alluring me with some mysterious hope and simultaneously threatening a crushing blow to pure reality. I am scared.

~

Our large home typically houses any and all visitors, and Hank and his 5-year-old son, Scott, have come for the convention. I would think nothing of it except that Jeannette (the wife of our former director) quizzed me vigorously a few months back.

"What would you ever want in a man?"

"I have never thought much about it, to tell you the truth," I confessed.

"Oh, come now; surely the thought has crossed your mind. There must be some qualifications you'd list in order of 'livability'; you know, what you could live with."

"No, actually, it's taken the starch out of me to simply live it as it comes, and I've never wound my focus down enough to pinpoint the criteria for the man of my dreams."

"Well, OK, then, how about right now? What do you think, off the top of your head, would be the most important qualities for him to have?" Jeannette sat with her red curls bouncing and her face a matching blush against the tan couch in our living room, pressing me against the backside of my marriage, insisting I outline what I would wish for instead of that. Slowly, complications were disengaged and scraped away, and for a fleeting moment I could see clearly the fundamental desires that would work for me.

"Spiritual. Yes, I would want him to love God and operate in that love. Second, I would want him to love me—and my children—and apply that love in ways I could recognize." I knew there was more, but I couldn't name the deeper thing in tangible words, or even thoughts, at the time. All the same, there trailed an obscure, yet particular, requirement, floating beyond what I could know then.

This strange questioning is registered faintly in back thoughts, yet surfaces unexpectedly when I see Hank walk away from our house the very first day he arrives. The sun has carved a circle of shade just beyond the steps. Our screen door slams shut, calling me to glance through our window to notice how broad his shoulders are as they hit the sunshine. His stride is deliberate, sure. No movement wasted.

I sense some vague sputtering in my body, more like a shooting feeling that leaps from my throat to my stomach. Standing in a cotton robe, hair frizzing in the summer heat, I continue to move the flatiron back and forth across the white shirt draped over the ironing board. I look mechanically down, then am drawn back to his walking-away form. Another part of me recognizes something: He is handsome. Manly, alive, and very handsome! That's all.

Just before the convention begins, the Applebys call me into their room. Filled with curiosity, I climb the familiar wooden stairs. I'd never been "called" into their room; always welcomed, but never "called."

Herb and Jean, matching white hair, matching tanned faces and arms, matching height, stand at the door to greet me. I feel their excitement before Herb speaks. "I want to talk to you about Hank, our new visitor. Did it ever occur to you that he came here to meet you? He's been divorced now for about two years." The words spurt out between the static of my own heart.

"He wants to remarry and is looking at possibilities for a wife and for a mother for Scott. Wilbur [the previous director and Jeannette's husband] suggested he come here to meet you."

I retreat into emergency automatic and stupefy.

Jean picks up the conversation. "Hank's the son of Marjorie Cook, the lady you stayed with during your vacation in Georgia a few years ago."

A tidal wave of *No* surges through me, engulfing the past, the future, the present. Surely they feel it too. I have to press against it to survive it. They ask me to think it over, say we can meet with him just to discuss it at 4:30, after the program. The clamor inside stifles the rest. I go deaf to anything more and leave the room.

The echo of my own "No" erupts, swelling to fill spaces within me I didn't know I had. This information slaps into my face so un-expectedly. No, I'm not ready! Forget the list. I want no such rela-tionship, not ever again in my life. No, this is the end of it.

Preparations for the gala meal steady me. On rote again, I count paper plates and silverware, break ice cubes free of their pigeon-holes, lug vegetables across the fields. What is the schedule, anyway?

> 11:00-1:00—Fellowship and frolic
> 1:00-2:00—Feasting to your fill
> 2:00-4:00—Speaker of the day

It is 2:05. We claim our seats in the rear of the tent—just inside the edge of shade—Kell on one side of me, Buff on the other. Dragonflies and butterflies hover over the gathering, magnetized, circling curiously to hear the speaker's report. The tent itself seems to reverberate as old hymns ring out with a common gladness. I sit braced against my future, yet curious about this man. He sits di-rectly in my line of vision, unobstructed by a single head, exactly six rows in front of us. Scott straddles his lap, facing him. Occa-sionally their glances meet, then each looks away. He strokes his son's head, kisses him, and strokes some more. Scott is used to af-fection, and Hank is used to giving it. This is evident. After a while Scott climbs down to play, building streets and stores in the dirt be-side the tent, then returns to board the lap for strokes again. Ques-tions bounce off the concave surface of my mind and float out into the air to recircle again under a new guise.

It's 4:15, and women, men, and children are milling every-where. Paper cups lie flattened into the dust, fires dwindle to ashes, musical instruments are tucked away in velvet cases for another time. So soon? Does it all have to end so suddenly? The girls are chatting with neighbor girls. *I should be carrying something, hauling something somewhere. It's time. I can make my own decisions. No one can force me to do anything I don't want to do. I am in charge of my life.* I head for the Applebys' room.

There we are, the four of us. Jean and Herb no longer match quite so well. She sits in the sunlight in her high, wing-backed chair in the corner of the room. He sits at their maple drop-leaf table in a ladder-back chair. The air seems stuffed with humidity, nearly choking me as I enter. I press forward to the only vacant seat, about four feet away from where Hank sits.

He looks different close-up. More handsome than I realized. Nearly black wavy hair grows in perfect outline to his strong face. His eyes are deep-set; he has a clean, yet weighted, look about him, and his defined jawbone holds the most beautiful smile I've ever seen. His brow is already creased almost to the depth of dimples that have been irresistibly placed on each cheek. His form is trim yet full of bulk. On some remote level I toss away the thought of being in his arms. I'm surprised to feel a trickle of sweat racing down the center of my back.

The Applebys make introductions, sorting out history for us into little tidbits of recognition. They flash brief clippings before us from our pasts, Hank's and mine, presenting them like tokens awaiting someone to claim them. It's very awkward. He sits with his back arched forward, an elbow resting on either knee, approaching casual, hands loosely folding together, then unfolding. His gaze alternates from his clasping hands to Jean, Herb, and me, then back to his own hands again. He clears his throat twice, trying to fill the silence.

I can't contribute a thing, and wait for something to call all this to order. Then I hear him begin, "I know Herb and Jean have told you why I'm here. So I'd like to begin by asking you if you would be interested in being friends?" He pauses briefly. "Just to get to know each other better—just as friends." The sound of his voice absorbs me, a male rhapsody pours forth with each syllable ringing across my eardrums in royal intonation. I imagine his inner spirit to match the magnificent sound of his voice and brace myself against it. He talks on and on. I don't hear most of what he says. My thoughts are tumbling around like a milkshake. I feel nauseated.

"Could I write to you?" I hear him ask.

"I need to think about such a decision," I stammer. "It's a big one for me." Yet a faint acceptance floats slowly across the commotion in my head. *He* could *write*. Trying to choke back the cotton billowing into my throat, I stutter, "You *could* write."

Through the fog the following morning, he is on his way back to Georgia, and I am glad to be alone again. The thoughts of becoming his wife, of mothering a son, immobilize me. The sum of all my inadequacies swarm like crazed vultures circling the threshold of my future, seeking to devour it. Full-blown details of every failure I've ever made march relentlessly through my mind. Encumbered with frustrations and disappointments of the past, I'm in no position to muster, either for inspection or performance, in that role again. It's just too much for me.

I keenly feel my deficiencies in wifely things. After 14 years in my first marriage, summoning every ounce of energy I possessed and developing every strategy I knew, I could not remedy whatever was wrong—whatever made it hell. It never righted itself. It still ended, despite my efforts to preserve it. I know it hadn't worked, but I don't understand why.

And my mothering abilities . . . My own daughters seem to claim all the maternal skill I have. How could I presume to gather another child under my wing? Discipline, training, guiding, caring for daily things like the clipping of toenails, and elbows off the table, and washing hands before eating, and saying "please" and "thank you," and on and on with those vital lessons. Never mind about the real issue—the exquisite art of loving a child. Loving a child with a zealous devotion. At all costs. No matter how I feel, or what I need. *This is as far beyond me as those dusted stars sprinkled across the New Hampshire heavens on a summer night,* I think as I slide between the sheets. No, I can barely function as a natural parent. It's absurd for me to think about trying it again.

Hank's strong presence, measured against my own lack of confidence, affirms this absurdity.

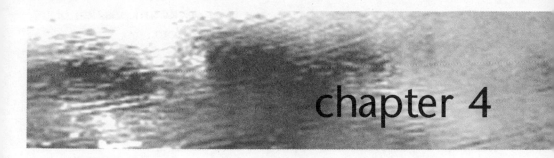

chapter 4

My Reluctance

Then something shifted within me and I felt courageous, trusting God to fix my inadequacies and make this thing come out right. So in spite of my fears, we gradually begin to recognize what we consider to be encouragement from God to go forward.

~

Gap Mountain produces a plateau of the sweetest wild blueberries, sweeter by far for their wildness, I'm sure. Long August Sundays beckon our entourage of 20 or more to indulge ourselves. Ancient bushes literally explode in blue profusion to flaunt themselves on our behalf. Baited, we carry five-gallon buckets and individual sacks of homemade granola up the steep, mile-high climb, brunching ourselves full once at the top. We spread across the hill much like honeybees stationing themselves across a rose garden, straightaway to the source, marvelously depleting the bushes to our own bucket, or our own mouth, whichever can be spared the most. By late afternoon we lug full pails down the hill to our waiting vehicles. That evening, dish-towel-covered cookie sheets fill our dining room table, where we sort and bag the blue treasure.

In the midst of all this the telephone rings. I answer.

"Yes, this is she. Yes, I got your first letter, but . . . Well, I'd been wanting to call you . . . to let you know that I'm not comfortable with writing. Please stop! It puts me in an awkward position of trying to explain to the girls who this letter is from."

I know it's creating the possibility of what I consider an impossible situation; my earlier courage wanes and I want out already. Hank promises there'll be no more letters. I trust this is the end of things. But several weeks later his name is brought up during our executive committee meeting. We need a man to direct our maintenance department, and Hank is well qualified.

"Is there any objection to his becoming part of our staff?"

I shudder inside, yet refuse to allow my personal life to interfere with a decision involving the rest of the community. We do need such a man. We do.

"No, no objections."

Don't they hear my inner howling against it? Yes, yes, objections everywhere! He must never come to this place! But my silent protests drill on without notice.

Hank and Scott do come to this place. He takes over the department with unexpected efficiency, winning the hearts of our relieved community. That voice, that male rhapsody that so caught me off guard at the first, begins singing solo hymns in our worship services. For a brief moment I think I must be dreaming. The smooth, velvet ribbons of that voice tug at my reserve. And he shares so freely from his new and vibrant Christian experience. I'm fascinated by his charm. Children love him. Like a magical relief, his refreshing presence flows abundantly into the dry pitcher of our diligence even as he grasps our aim, our industries, and our mission.

The chapel retains a kind of reverent beauty, carved intricately with curves and swirls of dark oak, floor-to-ceiling windows bending to an arch at the top, and a stone fireplace serving as a backdrop for the podium. Four years ago we seemed to have claimed a spot on the second pew, my girls nestled on either side of me. This Saturday morning is no different. We use the time for snuggling into each other.

Kell and Buff and I have been together since the beginning, even before the divorce. Cooking, gardening, laughing, crying, working together. They're enough; they're all I can manage. The speaker wagers on, and I feel Kell slip her hand into mine. Outside, a million leaves flip backward into a matte gray-green with the brush-width of wind. No, I don't need to muddle our lives further.

From a distance I watch him, noticing how he relates to authority, to young people; how he moves among the folk. He catches my eye from the next room after vespers one evening. He is clustered in a group of three or four, tossing his head back in a laugh that engages his whole spirit, one hand resting atop a little blond head reaching to just the height of his hip. I watch him with my heart and wonder to myself what it would be like to be his wife. I wonder how safe he would be. What he would demand of me. I wonder about everything.

Crossing the same paths, moving from place to place, attending the same functions, I avoid all possibility of personal connection with Hank. Yet I hear the irrepressible talk, the notion of Hank and me together—like a special ornament adorning the silver-blue garland of gossip draped now across the campus, falling into soft scallops here and there. Are you ready to begin dating?

By late October, winter engulfs us without warning. Snow buries any hint of a garden, and mayfly eggs are frozen beneath fallen leaves. Down the backside of the mountain (one of our favorite walking trails), Childs' Pond is covered with rippled ice, lacing the surface from shore to shore. Tall evergreens stand etched against a creamy-white, lilac sky. I have come to believe this place emits a consolation to worries, a balm to disturbances, a kind of altar where the soul can hear itself unfolding, tracing far back to where the wild rooting of a person first took place.

Nothing in life has prepared me for the depth of this decision. The misaligned episodes of my early years have left me off kilter, somersaulting from one event into the next, staggering a step or two in between to discover which way to lean next time. It's been shaky, always weighting myself heavier toward safety, fearing the fall from the edge of wherever I am. This is the first time I have been slowed to even keel, and any strong wind might blow me off course. I'm a novice at sound decisions.

Scripture verses seem to ring through my thoughts: *He forgives all my sins and heals all my diseases; He redeems my life from the pit and crowns me with love and compassion. He satisfies my desires with good things, so that my youth is renewed like the eagle's* (Ps. 103:3-5). *All* my sins! *All* my diseases! And "crowns me with love and compassion"! Such promises stacked up against my entire life. His Word following the seams of history, converging down to one small point in time: the present—now. This pivotal moment. Landing squarely at my feet in an instant when the full burden of the past must somehow merge toward a brighter future.

The question has been suspended long enough. Escalating tensions permeate everything I do. Am I destined to remain a single parent, or will I ever be a candidate for marriage again? Specifically: Will I *ever* be interested in getting to know Hank?

Leaning hard into the familiar tide of anxiety I persuade myself, *I could just try it. If I don't like it, I can quit. And God says He will help me become a good wife and good mother. Or is that the one thing that is too hard for Him?* Stabbing the guide stick into the air, I prod forward into unknown territory. Balance. Sanity. Maturity. I have no awareness of the tiny interior person I bring with me.

It's the Wednesday evening before Thanksgiving. Snow packs into a rosy, purplish outline against the roadways. Drifts are already waist-high. An aura of lavender is shedding lavender stars onto the snow. I can see it all from my bedroom window where I pace back and forth. The girls are busy with Thanksgiving favors, cutting and pasting red leaves that fade to a border of gold—burnt-orange ones, some tipped with sienna, others still revealing their green veins of spring.

They think I am busy, too, with Thanksgiving things. Instead, I'm busy packing my previous life into a bundle that's small enough to lift and toss into the night sky so that again I can begin chiseling my own inscription of a happier life. Reluctant, yet committed to my resolve, I'm ready to encounter Hank, to let him know that I am willing to date . . . Just to get to know him better.

A wool plaid scarf wrapped twice about my head, its fringes catching damp bubbles from breath chilling on the spot, muffles all remains of resistance. I head out the door and march diligently forward into the purple skyline turning black. I follow the snow path to Coopers' back-door light, where Hank is staying, while the community, who had so vigorously egged me on, is now preoccupied with their own holiday business. At last, standing in the icy night air, I face the front door of his residence and knock a slow, determined knock.

No answer. It is a precarious moment. Maybe this is not right. I *could* turn around and simply head back up the hill. Not a single soul would ever know I'd even come this far, and that would be the end of it all. I could go on in my simple world on automatic, undisturbed and safe.

A shiver of a moment later I hear footsteps, and the door is pulled open. A warm cone of light—a family-kind of light—empties into the darkness. Chuck, the director, greets me warmly, a surprised and knowing smile erupting across his face.

"Come on in. I'll be happy to find Hank and tell him he has a visitor."

chapter 5

Our Wedding

Oh, the simple but beautiful wedding day takes place! We're in our finest, though humble, attire. The feast is prepared; the chapel flowered. The main characters are standing in place, and the music is about to begin. We'd learned so much through past failures; now we hoped we could become a truly "blended" family.

~

Trudging crystal paths in a fairyland of evergreens and fresh snow, Hank and I gradually lower our shields and serve up our secrets to each other. The mystified childhoods lodged in our own perceptions; the private and single corridors of our adolescent years; the puzzling bent of our own inclinations; how we actually blundered through our poor choices, and yet survived to speak of it now. I utter my own story, pathetically, shamefully, as though it happened to someone I once knew intimately a very long time ago but no longer know at all. We're measuring each other against the lens of our own experience, assessing if, in fact, we can with whole heart accept the other's motive and decision at critical junctures, then at last compare the end results. I seek to discover the culmination of all these episodes: the person I face today. Is there a divine cord here, weaving between our lives, lacing us together in the future?

too hurt to love

A slow revelation is unfolding during our daily walks across the mountain. We feel ourselves branching out from this trial time, this practice family. Encompassing our three children within preliminary boundaries, we notice our blended image and how it ranks against fellowship with the community at large. Trying this "family" on for size, so to speak.

I laugh with new freedom at his jokes, question him mercilessly about minute details I trust will clue me into his character, providing a margin of safety against the years I haven't known him. Always, always, we tell each other, we're ready to stop this alliance if we ever think the obstacles seem too overwhelming.

The ribbons of our lives intertwine remarkably well, however. Born in the mid 40s, we know about the rural poor, poor for one reason or another. We know about playing as children in old copper washtubs on the front lawn (clad only in underpants), pressing buttercups beneath our chins to reveal the "butter secret." We've anticipated and relished Sunday chicken dinners and dined on fried bologna (cut partially to the center into bologna wheels), and delighted in overnight visits to our grandparents' home. We remember the discovery of television. We know Elvis and the world of "white sport coats and pink carnations," all ending in broken dreams. Our backgrounds dovetail together; our goals are identical. Easily honest about our histories, we're savoring the glut of similarities.

Along with the mental and emotional integration come occasional flashes of flesh and bone. Often, in the quiet pockets of an afternoon when the momentum of work subsides for brief moments, I find myself daydreaming. Simple joys pop into consciousness like cool, white sheets covering two bodies turning together in the privacy of night. More in my mind than in actuality, I can't deny that I wonder at the touch of his hand, the feel of his arm around me, or the full weight of his body against me. How warm is he? How strong? How soft is his skin? What does he smell like close-up? I mostly push these thoughts back into a file marked "Not now" and venture forward, self-contained.

Yet I remember the night of his first touch. We'd been out with a large group from our community on an extremely frosty winter evening. The old van was crowded with warm bodies and steamy breath, each of us a mass of shivers and chattering teeth, cold to the bone. I huddled on the seat with Kell on one side, Buff on the other. The whole group was singing loudly, trying to warm the air with our own sound. In the darkness I could see both his hands reach out toward mine. He instantly engulfed my shivering hands in his huge warm ones and rubbed my fingers and palms, briskly drawing the blood from my heart, racing down to the fingertips, rushing toward him. He certainly had his way of whispering to my soul.

We're well into a possible future when he confesses that he'd come to his own conclusion that very day before Thanksgiving. After several months without any indication of reciprocal interest from me, he had resolved to give his notice and move on to another position by the end of that day unless he received some indication of my willingness to begin a relationship. Had I waited another day our paths would never have crossed so intimately. I had to wonder if there is some divine clock that times us precisely together in the cycles of life.

Red satin hearts trimmed with doilies and cupids cut just so float suspended from the mobile overhead. The clear plunking sounds of a piano concerto decorate the night. We're sitting in my garden-view office, slow-drinking mugs of black currant tea. Snow is falling, big flakes and slowly. We've been together all day. I don't want to let myself "fall in love." I've buckled up against it, presenting a carefree air most of the time, but in spite of my resolve, I like having someone in my life—especially someone like Hank.

We stop our talk for a while and just sip at the tea. I feel his eyes on me, scanning the face he already knows so well. Then a deep notion surfaces: he is moving through the years ahead of us, taking me with him. A few moments later he begins with the pulp of an utterance.

"We've covered a lot of ground together, haven't we?" Just a tinge of a smile crowds his expression, that voice rhapsody lying like a span of velvet, catching piano droplets as he speaks. He takes another sip and puts down his mug. Taking both my hands in his, he turns his face directly into mine and pauses, as though the depth of winter is listening to him. "I want you to be my wife. Will you do that?"

How many nights have I lain awake, unable to sleep over this matter? Promising myself permission to let it go, to be swept away with the luxury of gliding without thought toward the nebulous acreage of sleep. I'd fought to break off each specific string that anchored me down to wakefulness. Sleep, where there's nothing churning in my mind, no details to attach to, just floating and yet more floating. Instead I found myself working on the thought, the firefly notions that relentlessly blink before me, hooking my attention. The formidable question can be delayed no longer. Would I? Could I? Deeper than the worded answer, the core part of me, the bud of who I am, knew I would say "Yes" whenever the time came.

His dark brown eyes are concentrated into aged wine, penetrating, sweet; and I force my gaze to stay there, matching his intensity. I am speaking with premeditated joy. "Yes, yes, I must marry you with all my heart."

In some small footnote of our promise we both know this will be our last attempt at successful marriage. Our last-ditch effort to make it in this world with another human being by our broken, but still lively, side. Born from the chip of a long-ago dream still held within our breast, the bubble of a golden room exists where a man and a woman can love each other; we see them laughing, hugging, supporting, and yes . . . yes, parenting together. We're still naive enough to believe in the possibility. Our mistakes had taught their lessons, books had enlightened us (surely by now we could put into practice the words on the page). Even friends had shared their advice, and we believe it's God's will that we marry—surely we can't ask for more. Our wedding is scheduled for March.

~

The chapel never looked so magnificent. White streamers are scalloped high along the oak panels, converging together in bows at the uppermost arch of the windows. Sunbeams stream from the universe into the solemn chapel just for this occasion. Piano pieces ripple with promises of hope and joy, while clusters of dressed-up folk mingle here and there, reveling in the certainty of their knowing about this marriage. Nodding their heads in unison: This certainly is a match!

Handmade dresses, fruit salad, special tea rolls, a single white, long-stemmed rose. A few outside friends and family and the entire school community attend our quaint, incredible wedding. Our three children find it nearly impossible to contain their excitement, yet throw sideways glances at each other, unsure of what to do with this new abstraction they are stepping into at the side of their parent.

The ceremony ended, I stand beside Hank, feeling myself glazing over. From the next room I hear the uneven cumulus of conversational tones rising and falling in varying swells. What have I done, taking on this man and his son? How will I be their happiness? Hank detects my stupor and nudges me gently into consciousness. I'm back.

He continues to greet the congratulators, shaking hands, receiving cheeks pressed against his cheeks; still stretching that glorious smile across his face. The children, too, somehow bear to keep their smiles wide. My own cheek muscles give way to the drifting of my mind. I stand numb, smile drooping, feeling myself slipping into automatic again.

We chug into our honeymoon with slips and starts. The car is not completely packed, and the children, tearful that we're leaving, beg to come along. We arrive at the cabin we've rented in Laconia, New Hampshire, and find that the hot-water pipes are shut off until we find the correct switch.

Shyly, I undress most of me. New pink nightgown. *Does he like pink?* I wonder. A few moments to myself in the bathroom, and we both come forward to endure the greeting. He looks me up and down, noticing the outline of my underwear. A muted smile creeps across his face, and I feel a defense rise from my toes. *So what?* I think to myself. But I smile back, realizing these too must go.

We crawl between the sheets and only begin to get to know the texture and temperature of each other's body. We keep talking, laughing, exploring until the morning comes, and we've become true lovers overnight. The act of breakfast, of walking, of suppers by the fire, of sharing and listening, of giving and receiving. And we sleep, we eat, we walk, and we make love to each other. Then start all over again, slowly accepting the early realizations that we are indeed husband and wife.

chapter 6

Reality

How is it that you can know a person so well, and yet not know him at all? Why is it that we truly unveil only after the wedding? Is the risk just too great before that? Is risk somehow lessened after the ceremony?

~

My rosy world turns lemon sour in a single day. As though a tornado were circling toward us, spinning round and round, collecting power for its final act of devastation. As if the very foundation moments of our marriage are being threatened. Our first few months together unravel my tightly knitted facade. I feel naked, embarrassed by the poverty I've just discovered in myself. Every insecurity I've ever buried surfaces.

I'm too fat! Why can't I be thinner? Cringing, I keep my bathrobe covering all I possibly can, flipping the light switch off before removing it altogether. I wish I were quick-witted, funny like Hank is. He loves music, loves to sing; I've never been able to carry a tune "in a bucket." (I've heard it said and know it's true.) Oh, to play an instrument, to accompany his singing! He loves to eat; I hate to cook.

Why didn't I know these things before we married? Why didn't my endless quizzing expose these differences? I compare myself to every woman I know and come up deficient. In every way I wish I were altogether better than I am.

too hurt to love

A witch's voice haunts me from a spoiled fairy tale. It comes unexpectedly, all shaky and grisly, sounding full of danger, coursing through whatever thoughts I might be thinking. *You are not enough. You are a bad mother. A bad wife. And Hank is just like your first husband—he'll abuse you too. It's what you deserve!*

My first husband. A shudder shoots down my spine, and I feel my stomach tighten instantly. I met him in high school in 1959. I was 14.

On our first date we went to see the newly released movie *Ben Hur.* In the dim flashes of light from the screen, I let him hold my hand. From that time, as he unfolded his sad story, it drew me in and begged me to rescue him. I found myself envisioning our future together, where every terrible item of his pathetic history would be righted. The dreams became tangled with my own needs, and before long I could see it all: a little cottage with a white picket fence, toddlers on a backyard swing, pansies by the mailbox, and the world rosy at last. Little did I know then that all the sweet talk that wooed me as a lonely teenager would become my own Edgar Allan Poe horror story, the beginning of an 18-year nightmare.

Swept into the cottaged future, I agreed to more dates that moved from slow dances and movies to violent arguments. In a fit of rage, he would literally assault me. In between rages he unloaded his misery into my heart, and I swallowed it up, feeling more significant than I had ever felt in my life.

He was so sorry after he'd hit me. He never knew why he did it. And his tears were so big. With his head bent low, cheeks wet with sorrow, he'd promise, "I'll never do it again." He'd assure me that I was "the best thing that ever happened to him." Ah, those words were his ticket into my life. I needed to be that to someone. Unable to tease apart the *love* from the *abuse*—or to recognize my option to separate them—we made wedding plans and were married in September 1963.

A shock came a month after our wedding. A police officer's husky voice vibrated through the telephone one late afternoon. He was explaining the hard facts that my husband was caught—he would be tried and convicted. I fumbled with the phone cord, staring straight ahead, feeling myself paralyze.

And so it happened. The court trial, his imprisonment, his release. It was over before it began—the cottage, the picket fence, the pansies—now just a shattered dream, gone like the dissolution of a comet in mid-orbit. Destroyed instantly.

It was 15 months later when he was released—just before Christmas. Kelly, my first baby, was 6 months old by then, and I was excited about his return, still not knowing how terribly distorted my perspective was. All the anticipation of our first holiday together dissipated into thin air as the rumblings between us intensified. I felt my insides freeze whenever I was in his presence. I barely dared breathe short, panicked breaths, even at midnight when he was asleep.

His fury was rampant after his return home. Prison had merely fanned the flames of his already uncontrollable rage, making the beatings prior to our marriage as nothing compared to those after his release. At the slightest provocation, he would lose all control. One incident exposes many that occurred through the years.

This time he was yelling and stomping toward me, reeking of the Winstons he smoked, that dirt-gray smell that stuffed a room until I couldn't breathe. By now I knew the bashing would bolt me out of consciousness, and wished it would hurry so the stopping would come. He lunged forward, straddling me as I lay where he'd thrown me across the bed, faceup. Always with those terrifying eyes feverish to kill his prey. Both hands scrunched my throat into a tiny string. I couldn't breathe . . . felt my eyeballs bulge from their sockets. My mind had to do something to survive it, so I waited—waited for the monster to weary of conquering. Waited without defense. Unable to move, speak, beg. Or promise never to do anything ever again.

He came so close to killing me in those days. I wonder whatever stopped him.

Winter finally began melting into spring, and daffodils burst into bloom. I saw their yellow buckets tipping just so in spring breezes, but lived removed from my senses as much as possible. Claiming the safety dazed living provided, I preferred to avoid the torment of reality. But I couldn't understand what I had done wrong—I was compelled to search my behavior: How could I prevent the inevitable beating?

My perception of myself, and how others should treat me, had become very skewed. As a 10-day-old infant, hospitalized with pneumonia, I had struggled to survive. Two years later, returned to the hospital for the same reason, my struggle continued. My very early years were spent in my grandparents' home, where my family lived with my two uncles and their families. Their teasing came without relief, and I soon understood that tickling was merciless and jokes were derrogatory. Resulting anxieties and tensions inadvertently affected my emerging perspective and developing self-worth. Childhood was lonely; I had no siblings, and both my parents worked full-time. Religion verified my feelings of worthlessness and served to distort my concept of God. As a little girl, my interpretations were shaped by unfortunate events, and I believed the bad things happened to me because I was bad.

So you see, years before my involvement with my first husband, I had thrown myself away, along with any sense of outrage—of right and wrong. It would have saved me now. It really would have saved me now.

But instead of protesting against his abuse or seeking escape, I simply surrendered to it. I let my body do the doing, shifting its torture to another time and place, where none of this mattered at all. In so doing, I inadvertently modeled for my children how to tolerate the intolerable—how to believe deep down inside that this was what I deserved.

~

I push hard against such horrible thoughts.

This marriage is different, I tell myself. *This husband is different.* What I don't know is that *I* am much the same—still unable to care for myself. The task of mothering Scott increases my torment. I've condensed the two roles of mother and wife into one. I'm unable to tease them apart; I check off "failure" for both. Somehow I'm convinced that Hank has married me only to acquire a mother for his precious son. And my worst nightmare has materialized: I'm unable to do the job. In the very first incidences of our daily routine, I feel the antagonistic rub of Scott's needs against my own.

For our first meal as a family I set the table, lining up our silverware at each place setting, but little Scotty requests a specific spoon. Not the one I've given him, but one of his own choosing.

Metaphorically, I hear a deeper message: "I want *my* mother!" and feel the sting. I don't understand his simple request or his need to control some part of his chaotic world. Instead, I bristle at the specificity and muffle my response. What I want to say is, "Take what I give you and be grateful for it!"

Scott's bedroom joins ours. I suspect he listens to all we say, that we have no privacy from him. The invasion I imagine is a curious one. In my mind I see Scott intruding upon Hank and me, on the union I wish for. Yet in my heart I believe that I'm the intruder, the newcomer to the strong bond I recognize between Scott and Hank. This father-son relationship established when, from birth, Hank completely took over Scott's care. Even as an infant, Scott went into the shower with Hank for his "bath." Hank fed him, took him back and forth to his day care and, eventually, was awarded custody of him. Scott, at just 2 years of age, convinced authorities— right in front of the judge—of his preference for his dad with intense outrage at being left with his mom.

Yes, Scott and Hank had a bond, a very evident bond. And I resented being on the outside of it. Early on, the tension is set in place, although I work to deny it.

~

The antiquated mansion we live in is divided into several apartments. Ours accommodates the whole north side. A green-roofed porch skirts the second floor and stretches the full length of our apartment, overlooking Mount Monadnock in the distance. Just beyond the French doors to the porch is our large, high-ceilinged bedroom. Reminiscent of New England history, antique scalloped moldings crown the entire room. Tall windows, sectioned by rotting wood dividers, separate the wavy glass. The fireplace provides our only heat.

A rust-colored, velour loveseat rests beneath the east window. It's here that Hank often sits reading, trying to dull the chronic ache of our union. I work, pace, read, and fret, waiting. Waiting for something to happen to make this ridiculous and terrible nightmare go away, wishing he'd say what I need him to say.

Our family carries an internal ruckus that seeps through on occasion. We are not blended. We are not peaceful. And we don't love each other. Neither parent is equipped to supply the mountain of needs that accumulate between us. Attempting to blend five different people into one family is a task that melds every need we have into a chaotic tapestry of pain that filters out again, magnified fivefold, to each family member. Kelly enrolls in a school in British Columbia, a convenient exit from our dysfunctional web.

Arguments prove most enlightening. Fueled with emotion and stripped of all safety measures, all manipulations, Hank and I ride the coil downward and plunge headfirst into honesty. The shouting, the silence, the nausea in my gut, then time to digest his truth and my own. All that to get beyond the fiction, all that to stand on common ground. As I see him dethroned from the pedestal I've placed him on, I realize I like the man.

In spite of the frenzy that curls about us, long winter nights offer the space to wrap ourselves up in each other's arms and lie close, the security of that embrace worth far more than the separation.

chapter 7

The Family

These first few months make it very clear to me that I am in trouble. But I am too ashamed to share the magnitude of my frustration with Hank or anyone else. In the quiet womb of Hank's family's home, I can't help remembering the births of my own children as I try to bring about this third birthing of my stepson as my own.

~

Hank often talks of his wonderful family—Grandma, Grandpa, the 12 children, and their children. He's created a fascination in me. Who are the people he comes from? A few days before our first Thanksgiving together I suggest we visit his family in Ohio. A chance to meet our children, their children. He's so proud of them that I want to belong to that family. I think it might start with introductions.

Unexpectedly, we hit a blizzard enroute, stretching the travel time of a usual eight-hour trip into 18 hours of vigilant driving through snow that instantly cakes against the windshield. At last we arrive in Crestline, tense and tired. The house is quiet in the wee hours, so we blindly feel our way through the kitchen, tagging onto the back of each other behind Hank to our upstairs rooms, and crawl between the sheets. Within moments Hank drifts into a deep sleep while I lie there feeling emptier than usual. Into the morning hours of this strange room I listen to the full, raspy sound of a train whistle hooting its arrival. Once the whistle stops, clanking wheels rotate round and round on the steel tracks, their tinkling sound fading off into thick silence once again. I hold my watch as far as my arm will reach into the beam of street light pouring through the window. It is 4:30 a.m.

An iridescent blue streak shines into an upper corner across the room. Widening my eyelids their full extent, I see the tiny rose-bouquets-and-vine-covered wallpaper peeling away from the corner, the ceiling plaster cracked and stained. A tear meanders down the corner, weaving back and forth before disappearing over the ledge of darkness. Closet doors are made of wooden slats, painted white, their black latch hinges no longer meeting their resting place. The oldness is everywhere—and I am curious. Did Hank sleep here before? as a child? with another wife?

Encased in blue solitude, I desperately explore how to birth a love for the grandson of this family by vividly recalling the births of my own children. Sharp, clear scenes from 1963 step into focus as if it were only yesterday. . . .

~

I am 18 years old and bona fide green. As a Catholic, birth control has never crossed my mind, despite the fact that I have just been married. Now I begin counting the days, frantically, wondering about the delay of my first menstral cycle since the wedding. Only a month into my marriage, and it has already begun to tumble apart. My husband has been sent to prison for a year and a half; I'm under a good deal of stress. Perhaps that stress has caused the delay. Or could I be pregnant? Was I, at this very moment, carrying a whole new person inside of me, even as her future was dissolving, right along with her parents' dreams?

Four weeks later, a pregnancy test comes back positive.

The next few months are a mixture of wonder and bewilderment. What am I waiting for? More than the undefined experience of labor, how *will* "mother love" work itself out in me? What will I feel for the lifeblood I carry inside? Will I feel anything?

When I was 5 I got Ellen, my first baby doll. I pushed her eyes into her head, leaving only black sockets to stare back at me. It's easy to remember how I'd practiced, in little-girl fashion, this "mother love." But *this* will be different; *this* love will bond me to a human child, *my* child.

I keep busy working full-time and preparing for this first birth. I cover an old bassinet with yellow cotton ruffles and paint a dressing table soft goldenrod. Three days before my due date, June 25, with mobility becoming more and more limited, I decide to begin my maternity leave and stay at home to wait. But waiting is getting the best of me. Four days later I decide to enter the hospital to have labor induced.

Finally, all these months of waiting will soon be over. I feel a tremendous relief at the thought of it. But it seems strange to be so calculated about it. It doesn't coincide with other stories I've heard about the beginning of labor, in which the husband escorts the mother-to-be into delivery. I feel as though it is my responsibility to get myself through this. I pack my bags, take my shower, and drive to St. Luke's Hospital.

I don't dare let myself feel the fear, the loneliness, that burns just beneath the mechanics of it. Instead, as I lie in the labor room, I concentrate on this child within me until the pains became severe enough to distribute my awareness into pockets of consciousness. Seven hours of black-and-white time, like in school rooms. Seven hours broken down into five minutes, seven minutes, many minutes of sweating, of writhing. Then, just after midnight, *she* is born.

I am spent from the work of it, every nerve and muscle collapsed, when unexpected waves of loneliness engulf me. I wish my husband were here, wish he could see her too. Tears run down my cheeks, in spite of my efforts to hold them back. Here is this wonderful moment, and he is not here to share it with me. How I long for him to hold me, to be part of this brand-new excitement that fills my heart. As if a door slams down in front of me, cutting off any hope—or even the wanting itself—I realize he can't be here. And there is nothing I can do to change that fact.

Nearly an hour later, the nurse enters my room with a tiny bundle wrapped in a receiving blanket, black hair sprouting out one end. She smiles at me, and I wipe my face, hoping she won't notice I've been crying.

How I have waited to hold this wee bundle in my arms! I pull back her blankets and am instantly struck with the tiny face looking back at me. I'll never forget this first moment. It is love at first sight, instantly, and yet slow grown over eons of generations that make us one. I sense a kinship to her conceived at the beginning of time. She is soft and ruddy and beautiful! Eloquent without words; all that perfectly brand new can be. Black hair outlines her flawless face and . . . She looks *so* like her daddy. Amid all my anguish I know I want—that I adore—this newborn girl.

Kelly and I learn together to be infant, to be mother. She mystifies me. Breast-feeding for hours, I feel grateful for time to hold her close; to gaze into her tiny, perfect face; time for rocking; for singing her off-tune lullabies with cherishing. Reverencing every whimper, grunt, and squeal, I crudely but diligently attempt to interpret her unspoken requests from baby world.

I lie in bed with her whole body lodged in the crevice of my forearm, staring at her satin fingers, satin cheeks. Sunshine spreads itself across the covers, piling shadows deep around us. Lace curtains parachute out, filled with a gentle northeast wind. And I wonder, what spirit keeps life beating within her? Who is she? Who will she be? I empty what love I have into her tiny being, cherishing her now, cherishing whomever she will become. I listen at odd hours of every night, just to be sure she's still breathing.

Then it's four years later. My life has gained a semblance of order. My husband and I have purchased two acres of land and built ourselves a three-bedroom ranch house.

November 1967 comes in cold and hard without warning. Early snow sloshes the earth to mud beneath our extra-heavy feet as we carry all we own into the unfinished house. Our challenged little family is stumbling along quite ungracefully. Falling, getting up, falling again. Still, we proceed to improve slightly, ever so slightly. Despite our condition, I want another child, want Kelly to have a sibling, someone who will understand what it's like to be our child, who can validate her worth just by her existence. Confident that she is such a special child, I want another.

One January midnight I conceive again. Not knowing for sure if it will be a boy or girl, I paint the room two shades lighter than robin's egg blue and hang crisp, white, ruffled curtains on the windows. Kelly's crib (which had originally been mine) would be perfect one more time.

Buff (her real name is Bethany) storms into my life on October 17, crying almost nonstop with a colic that won't quit. As if she were still a part of me, I cradle and soothe her, days chasing into nights of walking, rocking, lullabying her into comfort. Her eyes follow mine as though she can look inside. In the velvet robe of long midnights I doze; she dozes. Rocking her during the sacred hours she spends in my arms, I covet her presence, treasure what I recognize as majesty, and the trailing fragrance of what I know will be my last baby.

When she is 4 months old, as if some quota has been met, the crying abruptly stops. From that moment on, Buff is a delightful, outgoing baby. But she too is vulnerable to our outrageous alliance and endures the terror in our home.

One evening she comes creeping down the dark-pined hallway, clad only in a diaper, unsuspecting, evidently looking for someone to talk to her. Instead, she sees me hurled through the air and splattered on the wall across the room. Even all these years later, I still hear her blood-curdling shriek spin through the house as she grasps what is happening.

My enraged husband storms out the door, and I lie limp in a heap on the floor, stunned. I can't think, can't feel. Where is Buff? I saw her coming, know she's taken in this scene. I drag myself across the floor to where she is frozen into position and gather her in my arms, rocking her gently back and forth, singing, "'Hush, little baby, don't say a word; Mama's gonna buy you a mockingbird.'"

~

Suddenly it is morning, and I realize I am 13 years older. My girls and I have survived those tumultuous years. We are in Ohio, visiting our new family, and the big house is bursting. There must be 30 people here already, family who live here and family who don't, and neighbors who wish they did. The aroma of turkey, dressing, turnips, and pumpkin pies lodges in the hallways and filters up to the bedrooms. Laughter erupts from clusters of people in every downstairs room. I sit on the edge of our bed, chenille bedspread balding beneath me, trying to recruit enough courage for this momentous tryst. And I feel myself shrinking down inside to a tiny, shameful dot. I want to go home.

too hurt to love

Instead, I tell myself this is where I belong, that everything will be fine, and hoist my whole body off the bed. I take it determinedly forward and descend the stairs to begin the painful art of mingling, still wondering how to make Scott my own.

My defects appear magnified in the presence of this family. Their quick humor leaves me dumbfounded—I can think of nothing to say. Their bond with each other is practiced and obvious. The teasing, the laughter, the loving they share stand in flagrant contrast with the isolation I feel. I spend the weekend shriveling emotionally and trying not to let it show. I know I'm unsuccessful. Quicksand surrounds me; I'm nearly to my waist in the stuff. Engulfed by fear, jealousy, self-hatred, I try to claw my way out, but my fingers merely dig tiny trenches that fill in quietly with more wet sand.

chapter 8

The Secret

Stepparenting, like a coin or magnifying mirror, has two sides. Flipped one way, its upturned surface displays the child; flipped the other, the parent alone is featured. The dilemma lies in the inability of the one to perceive the other. Yet the expected difference in maturity is a crucial factor. The single most significant gift that can be given is for the parent to recognize and respond appropriately to the child's perception. How impossible this is to do when the parent, in her middle years, finds she's inadequate, empty, and, in ways, still a child herself!

I was deadlocked. I knew it. Others knew. They didn't like it. I didn't like it. Yet I was unable to change, and began to feel hopeless.

~

I'm enlisted into the role of mother during the second act, breaking into Scott's life after it's already begun. I'm unsure of how much to do for him or to let him do for himself. Baths, toenails, teeth brushing, duties? What was his own mom like? At 6, exactly what does he know?

I've taken him on, the decision settling like lead on my heart. Feelings of love will come in time, I tell myself. Careful practice will polish the partnership beautifully. But is it not true that birthing a son requires an act of union between his parents over the matter? The union. The union, I know nothing about.

too hurt to love

~

It's late summer, and the months have been interesting. We avoid discussions about Scott or my turbulence, while Hank walks a tightrope, guardedly reserving his affection for Scott lest his displays of love incite further uproar from me. He teeters on the edge of both relationships while denying, when possible, the terrible rupturing taking place in his own heart. Meanwhile, on our end of things, we work at attaching at every possible juncture. Early-morning walks are a mutually gratifying experience and continue despite the weather.

This morning silver streamers dance downward from the taupe ceiling overhead, splashing onto the pavement where thousands of iridescent rain-flowers hit the ground, forming water petals. At each acorn or pebble rivulets feather out from point of impact into liquid fans coursing into brown velvety trenches nearly three inches deep. From an eagle's distant view, the current resembles a massive stretch of wide-wale corduroy, pleated together at one central point.

The smell of water invades our nostrils, the background drumming like a tamed Niagara. My arm is knotted into Hank's elbow as we trudge through a path of continuous puddles. Feigning dryness, our golf umbrella presses up against the downpour. The sound of our soaking wet pant legs flaps against our boots. We talk of light things, things we can find to coincide, things that avoid our children's issues, our differences, the critical zones. The day is good. Too good to be spoiled.

I have office work to keep me as busy as I choose to be. Kell and Buff attend the small school on campus and leave before 8:00 each morning. Hank bends to our lifted cheeks, bestowing a quick goodbye kiss, and seems lighter as he closes the door behind him. This leaves Scott and me to each other.

We approach the day disjointedly, starting and stopping at odd moments, never in harmony. I always feel as if I am out of sync with him. Dawdling into his clothes each morning, poking his way through baked millet and raisins, playing puppet with the dish towel draped over each bowl or dish, his creativity spills over to ease the offenses he must endure.

Autumn reels in upon us, casting crimson shadows across the

56

massive garden below. Half buried by dead leaves and spent vines, vegetables lie scattered across the field, mirroring an apricot sky. A chill in the air dimples our skin, vaporizes our breath. Christmas conversations spin out thin threads of joy, promising new plaid jammies for a little boy, a white nylon scarf with old-rose and baby-aqua angels patterned on it for a young lady, a recorder for a budding musician.

Worthy of mention here are the episodes of pleasant times when Scott and I actually play together. Traditionally, the kitchen is dusted in whole-wheat flour as proof of forthcoming Christmas cookies. I'm forcing the wooden spoon into the powder crumbling below, turning it into dough. I apportion a pile for Kell and Buff for after-school cookie cutting, but know Scott is eager to taste his first attempts. He stands with his back to me, both arms lifted in the air as I tie the smallest apron I can find securely above his protruding tummy and under his armpits. He stares at the balloon of blue and white checks in front of him and smooths it flat against himself. Mounting the red kitchen step-stool, he examines the cookie cutters to discover what's available and is ensconced for the afternoon.

I roll the dough a quarter of an inch thick and show him how to wield a rolling pin. He follows suit, then carefully presses the cutter with both arms weighting straight down upon it. With the same care, he drags the dough into lopsided shapes—Christmas trees, reindeer, and wild angels, boarding the sheet bound for the oven. Two hours later, he's decorating. Pastel green and pink icing, silver balls, and chocolate sprinkles. More on his face than the now-dimpled cookies.

Gradually, cooking lessons expand into measuring, counting, and reading his own recipes. In the same way, through the years, we do waffles, oatburgers, cashew loaf, spaghetti dinner from scratch (including homemade sauce), and many breakfast dishes—baked oatmeal, fruit crisp, and blueberry pancakes. Eventually, he builds a recipe collection, and I feel grateful for the moments when he's entertained.

I try to make sense of my own paradoxical feelings about him. I know he should be held and mirrored and laughed with, allowed to explore and return to a safe place. Yet mostly I go through the motions on rote. I compel myself to manifest appropriate behavior much of the time. It's as though I'm forging parallel paths ahead of me, one recognizing this little boy with love, another festering a growing resentment I can't fathom for the life of me. I'm not comfortable discussing it with Hank, but I know he knows.

Christmas comes and goes, and the last carol fades away. The typical blizzards hit hard, lowering a puff of fresh white padding over the garden hill, and Scott and I are lured. He remembers last winter, stretching on our backs as tall and wide as we could, waving our arms and legs flat against the ground, fanning angels into violet shadows of snow.

"Mommy, it's here, it's here!" he screams into our bedroom early one morning. His hair peaks and flattens from his soundness of sleep, his eyes barely widened yet, but from his window he knows this time the snow is deep enough. His voice is fuzzy, trying to hold back the loudness. "Can we slide? I know where the wooden sled is," he assures me. "Can we?"

I rub my eyes and crawl to the window. Sure enough. The stuff is here. And I did promise we would ride it early before others packed it in too slick or crowded us out. He's flushed pink and warm from sleep. "OK, OK," I say, sighing loudly, annoyed at my own promise.

He dashes to his room with newfound speed and climbs into overalls and sweatshirt, altogether forgetting to dawdle. "Let's hurry before the others come!" he warns.

I too climb into warm clothes and let him lead me out the door and down the stairwell. He's in his blue snowsuit. His red knit scarf is spun tightly about his head, barely revealing two hazel eyes blinking against the wind. We drag the old wooden sled, the one with steel runners, out into the fresh fallen powder.

"OK, Scotty, it's our turn!" I toss the words to him through the moist sapphire air. Climbing on first, I pat the space between my legs. "Right here; this is where you sit." He wiggles himself as close as possible.

The morning air waits with quiet anticipation while we push off, smoothing the powder as we go, gaining momentum by the second. Tiny broken flakes of snow tap gently against our cheeks, and the violet of morning washes into the ashen sky. Early is the only way to do a hill of virgin snow.

These sweet times make the bitter all the more unbearable.

58

chapter 9

The Dish

Leftover issues never go away by ignoring them. I wanted to love Scott. I decided to love him! I pretended to love him. Yet, even when for brief interludes I seemed actually to feel something close to it, my resentment always took over and left us devastated again. I could not understand why loving this child was beyond me, or why he triggered me so violently.

∼

July's lemon haze pours through the huge glass windows encasing my garden-view office, which overlooks the landscape below. It's now an organized patchwork of assorted colors—olive, chartreuse, gold—random squares dotted with flecks of crimson. I watch the students from my perch as they haul buckets of freshly picked corn, tomatoes, and broccoli across the roadway into the large kitchen of the plain house with plain furnishings. Two young women in their late teens squat in the dirt, their sweaty hands working expertly to thin out new shoots of carrots and beets. Another young woman hacks away vigorously, both hands whipping the hoe, at mounds of new potatoes in her attempt to loosen the soil without gouging the goods.

It must have been at least 20 minutes ago that I'd completed my report on Charles, a new student who's just arrived, but I stall, my elbows on the old oak desk, cupping my face in my hands, and stare out the window. How long have I been here, daydreaming, escaping, dallying at the sight of this colonial plantation, reminiscent of a time when families knew each other, worked together—cared?

I yield my attention willingly to the outside activity until I'm yanked into the present moment by the crashing sound of china shattering into a million pieces on our kitchen floor just outside my closed door. Suddenly I am back to where I don't want to be. The sound jolts my attention to this family. My family. And *Scott*. The dreaded rumble is boiling over somewhere deep inside, way below emotion. I shuffle forward in my mind to the present, collect my body into its familiar, pompous authority, and head for the door. All is quiet. No dishes being wiped, no movement in our tiny kitchen at all.

He's waiting, hiding.

Opening the door, I step over the dish towel, thrown in a clump on the floor, and tiptoe among the demolished china. Instantly, I recognize the tiny bits of brown and blue, summer and winter. *Oh, no, not that dish!*

The brown-and-blue picturesque Limoges china Nana had given me herself before she ever got sick. The gift had come at a time in my life when I didn't think or care much about antiques or their beauty or value, nor did I think much about family. I didn't realize then, when I was 14, the profound impact "family" has on the development of a human being.

The rectangular soup bowl—blue snow scene on one side, brown summer scene on the other (unique and chipless)—was truly a treasure to me. On that day many years ago, I'd accepted the heirloom gratefully, clutching it to my heart, then packed it away, dreaming of the day I might serve a dark-brown beef stew in it in her honor.

I look for Scott, but he's nowhere to be found. I call his name. No answer. I call again, and still no answer. "You'd better come out here and help clean this up!" I warn, marshaling myself into a display of calmness, but the boiling brims to the top between my threats. I have all I can do to hold it back, to bury it. I want to shake him and throw him against a wall and shout, "Why did you break my beautiful dish? How dare you do that to my treasure! I want you *gone!* You don't belong here! Get out!" These are the words that toss violently inside me, that I must not let out.

I call his name again and again, warning all the while about how he must come and clean up this mess. Once through the kitchen, I let my steps fall heavily across the living room floor and into his bedroom. Thundering against his hiding, I pick up speed, looking under his bed, behind his bureau. Where would a 6-year-old boy go when hunted?

At last I see him. Huddled in the closet, crouched down to inches, peering up behind squinted eyes, trying not to breathe. He's waiting for the lion to devour him. Without a word I grab him by the shoulder and escort him into the kitchen, then hand him the gold plastic dustpan and brush. Instantly, he's down on his hands and knees, performing his small brushstrokes across the worn linoleum in silence, sweeping broken heirloom pieces into the cracked dustpan. Slowly, slowly he works, half looking at the floor, half looking up at me. I stand tall beside him, watching, not daring to utter one word lest I scold him with the uproar I feel inside.

I could kill him in this moment! The injury is unforgivable! I have no room to accommodate that kind of injustice. He should never have done such a thing! I watch him as one watches a leopard imprisoned behind bars at a zoo. I, the observer; he, the caged.

He is so small for his age, still carrying baby skin into his sixth year. Little dungaree overalls are caught at the bib front by straps reaching from one back-paneled V, pants length rolled up at the cuff, a red-and-navy plaid flannel shirt tucked into them. Black high-top sneakers betray stones kicked ahead of him and trudging through acres of garden dirt. His oval-shaped head, ears lying closely behind his temples, is crowned with just enough brown curls (one spirals always onto his forehead in a determined way) to be envied by any girl later on, when they might notice. Hazel eyes (like mine) rest atop rosy cups of skin, a miniature nose carries five brown freckles, and his first teeth sit like a row of corn, even and matching along top and bottom. His father's dimple is captured in his right cheek, nudging up close to a smile that lights up the whole country of his face. The smile always catches me off guard; it's totally unexpected. It comes at moments when he should have no reason to smile. I don't know what brings it, or why, or when.

Now there is no smile. "What will you do to me? Whatever it is,

too hurt to love

I will find a way to survive it," I read as the bulletin of the moment. As if he were crawling through a mine-filled area in Vietnam waiting for the explosion, unsure of where to next stretch his tiny body, he works silently, performing obediently, in the land of terror.

Horrified by the slap of my own reaction, I know something is terribly wrong. How could I be this angry over a dish?

chapter 10

Misconnection

I felt endless frustration. Despite the resentment that brewed within, part of me was deeply concerned for Scott. I made a million attempts to conquer myself.

~

In Tennessee a year later (1982), Hank is teaching industrial arts and Bible at a private Christian school. Buff attends as a student, and Kell has made her escape to British Columbia. Detached now from outside obligations, I determine to get ahold of myself and this secret dilemma.

How I strain to observe Scott—his mimicking of Hank's every move; the depth of his voice, the way he crosses one leg horizontally over his lap, his confidence in knowing about every player in baseball or football—and the resentment I feel pulsing with every beat of their connection. I'm so ashamed to admit this to a soul. Yet among the assorted jealousies, a sincere compassion for Scott and his own mom, Roberta, swirls intermittently. I write letters to her, enclosing snapshots of Scott in his routine day, explaining his life to her. An attempt, it seems now, to enhance *their* connection, since the one Scott and Hank already have seems to tear me apart, and my own bond with him is impossible. I'm absolutely sure he needs an attachment to someone, yet I work against it wholeheartedly. My letters, trying to present a balance, go something like this:

August 23, 1982
Dear Roberta,

I know you must wonder how Scotty is doing—you must miss him very much. I'd like to fill you in on how he is and how he spends his day. We have a schedule each day and try to complete our household duties quickly and thoroughly. He works a good part of the morning, doing odd jobs with me or by himself, then usually plays in the afternoons. As far as chores go, he dries the dishes, sets the table, empties the garbage, puts away our empty jars from canning, helps preserve fruits and vegetables, shells peanuts from which we make our own peanut butter, and folds clothes. On Thursday mornings we do our housecleaning, and he cleans his own room, vacuuming and dusting, then dusts the living room and empties wastebaskets. [Since I didn't know how to play, work of one kind or another occupied our time together.]

He has a little pool in our backyard here where he can play on hot days. I think his bike is still his favorite pastime, though. We live at a Christian school located on 350 acres. Only about 100 acres are under cultivation, and there are several dirt roads reaching from field to field and house to house, giving Scott some nice, flat ground on which to ride. He really enjoys this and sometimes comes home sweating from head to toe, but after a cool drink he's ready to go right back out again.

I am sending this picture of Scotty making waffles in our kitchen in New Hampshire one day last winter. He often sings while he works! Can you tell he's whistling? [Like a baby bird waiting for the worm, his lips protrude to construct a hoop of a whistle.]

In this picture we are raking and cleaning. We collected this big brush pile from surrounding clutter; now it's been moved to the dump. Scott likes this kind of work, and we do quite well together [more my wish than his reality]. *It provides opportunity for us not only to accomplish something and enjoy that satisfaction, but to visit together. He talks continually about absolutely everything. His questions are interesting—sometimes simple, and sometimes quite challenging.*

He has a real interest in people, be it history, or family, or people right around us here. He's also very interested in nature and has several books on different nature subjects. He'll often shoot facts to me about this whale, or that Australian animal, or this insect he's just discovered. He remembers what he reads and comprehends very well.

We will keep in touch,
Cindy Cook

Although he played and read and questioned and grew, and there appeared a semblance of normalcy, all of that was undergirded by my obsession with his performance. I wanted him to be what I thought he should be and strove to shape him so. I had to perform a certain way, and Scott had to perform a certain way.

Everybody had to perform a certain way.

Although frustrated and disappointed in myself, I continued to mold Scott according to my plan. He cleaned vegetables, picked up lawn sticks, and dried dishes. I scanned the area for whatever he missed, ready to pounce on him when he didn't complete the task to my satisfaction. I was obsessed with *his* behavior. Though I hated what *I* was doing, I felt powerless to stop.

During this time I read to Scott daily, and he devoured the stories as eagerly as I did. *Pilgrim's Progress* was our favorite, especially the story of Christian flung to the earth by powerful Apollyon's attack, "through darts as thick as hail" in Immanuel's Land. Flattened and weary, Christian summons every ounce of strength, rising up one last time to deliver the final blow, at last defeating his enemy and winning a mighty victory. Every vibration of that scene pulsated through our beings as we cheered Christian on.

Kneeling together, night after night, we implored Christian's God on behalf of our family, our friends, *ourselves.*

chapter 11

Home Schooling

Looking back, I can see a repetitive pattern. When overwhelmed, I redouble my efforts. Since mothering Scott overwhelmed me, I became his teacher also.

∼

It's 1983, and we've moved from Tennessee to Vancouver, Washington, where both Hank and I have been offered positions with a child development center. I become personal secretary to the president, and Hank manages their plant operations. A year and a half later, we sense a direct injunction for me to stay at home and devote myself to mothering and home schooling—two very lofty, yet obscure, goals. Despite the odds, we're convinced this is the best opportunity for our children.

A quilting business slowly evolves for me that's modified through the years to focus on sweatsuit designs. This creative avenue serves me well and actually pays for future dreams. For now, hoisting the task of home schooling both Buff and Scott upon my shoulders is overwhelming, and I stagger under the weight of it.

Today they each sit at their desks, attacking arithmetic with the gusto of a snail forced to cross the Sahara Desert. I sit in a caned-back rocking chair in the living room, waiting for them to finish, lost in reflection. The gray shadows of leaves move to their own rhythm in the white-windowed light across the carpet, a reflection of an outside dance. The clock strikes 2:00. From where I sit, I can see Scott leaning forward on his desk, his head cocked sideways on one elbow. His face contorts in puzzlement; he scratches his nose without lifting an eye from the page. Bored, helpless, his pencil moves in endless circles. *When will this day be over?* he wonders. *How many more must I endure?*

By 2:30 their work is turned in and checked over.

"But Scott, you have not completed these five problems! What's going on here?" I demand.

He stands before me, his eyebrows rising in unison with his scrawny shoulders in a shrug as if to say, "I don't know, whatever do you mean?"

My frustration peaks. "Well?"

He still can't produce a reason he doodled away math time making airplane circles across the page.

"Is it something to do with NASA?" I query, at my wit's end.

He dares to crack the beginning of a smile, and I feel my own brow cross into a deep-set frown, my neck muscles stiffen. "Now, listen here, Scott, these are to be done before you go to the zoo with us tomorrow. Do you understand that?" I hate threatening him, but I do it all the time. I don't want to ruin our plans or leave him home, but I'm down to zero with no leverage left.

The next morning I look for the work. There is none! Meeting him in the hallway, I notice he is still short for being 9. "How about it?" I say, waiting for him to flip the finished page from behind his back to surprise me.

Instead, with a toss of his head he turns around and saunters away, saying, "I've already been to the zoo anyway!"

So much for leverage. I don't understand him. If the conjecture is true that whoever you have a connection with is a mirror for you, and the deeper the connection, the stronger the mirror, then I'm stumped about the kind of connection I have with Scott. If, indeed, this conflict mirrors a part of myself I am uncomfortable with, and the situation won't change until I admit and accept all aspects of myself, then how and when do I get to that unresolved part?

Scott and I are opposite in so many ways. From my perspective, Scott is a free spirit. He enjoys "being," not doing. I call him lazy.

He's unconcerned with details; it's the overall gist that sends him on his way. And on his way he goes, propelled to do whatever he sets out to do. Nothing stumps him. He doesn't strive. He has a sense of humor. He's in control.

I, on the other hand, am bound. "Doing" is my habit. I'm serious. Thorough. Diligent. Moving in and out of details, whether they matter or not. How can it be that he mirrors me? Or I, him? I don't consider that any kind of mirroring fit. In fact, he appears to be my antithesis. We are like opposite ends of magnetic poles constantly resisting connection.

One thought persists in low rumble: Is it possible that I am addicted to my role? Have I cast myself a script with rigid boundaries that imprisons me? Is the chronic cycling of my waves of hatred a negative way to stay attached? I can well relate to the cycling, but it baffles me. Other doubts occasionally flash into consideration. Do I treat Scott the way I felt treated myself? Or do I really want to *be* more like Scott? Am I like him, somewhere deep inside? Perhaps long ago? Did my power get rebuked and buried, and his is still out there waving triumphantly above the din, like the flags he loves so, for all the world to see?

I hold these speculations secretly to myself. As his stepmother and teacher, the years have brought me no closer to discovering the key to this child or to my own heart.

chapter 12

The Beating

It is truly painful to write this chapter. And all chapters.

∼

I am so far away from where I want to be with Scott. I guess at correct behavior and artificially create it from day to day. At other times the boil comes spilling out all over us, and the devastation remains for days, for years.

I will never forget one of those days. Fresh, dry laundry, just in from the clothesline, is strewn across the couch. Underpants are thrown on top of each other against the back cushions. Undershirts on the right front corner, shorts on the left, and T-shirts hung half on and half off the front center cushion, draping down to the floor. Categorized by types, the child had begun the duty. But somewhere during the task dish towels had become flags and socks turned into gloves with which to do battle. And his favorite Bible character, David, is engaged with Goliath. One leg straight out behind him, the other bent sharply at the knee in front, he is positioned toward the enemy, cutting through the dead living room air with a curtain rod sword. With uncanny deftness, he wields several loud swishes back and forth against the enemy.

From the kitchen I hear a low-slung growl slide from between his teeth, background sound to my peeling potatoes for supper. I look up from my peeling, the muddy potato grit dripping from my hands. His eyes are fixed on the monster, Goliath, as surely as if his life were at stake. For a brief moment two notions swirl in my head, each clamoring for rank. The first: What an imagination! The child is actually starring in a drama he has written, produced, and directed. I am, for an infinitesimal flash, truly glowing with pride.

But then the other thought shakes my whole body into a rage and I bellow, "What *are* you doing? You are *supposed* to be folding those clothes, you lazy little brat! You always do this! You never stick with it. Get it done; get it done! You play instead of getting it done."

Suddenly, in brackets of thought, *I'm* the one brandishing the double-edge sword toward my own conscience, flipping it rapidly back and forth from justified to guilty, from justified to indicted.

In this excruciating moment I succumb to the intensity of my own inner clamor and throw down the peeler and tear across the room, not after the monster, but after the hero. I yank the curtain rod from him before he realizes I've even noticed him, before he's aware that I've entered his drama. Without a margin of time, I'm screaming down on him, my face contorted into a red leather drawstring purse, eyes lost in the folds. My fury lashes out savagely despite my efforts to hold it back. In an instant I lift the rod as far back as my arm will go, gathering all my energy into one swing of it, and propel the thing forward, down onto his bottom, feeling the metal flail into his skin. The abrupt ending stuns me. A flash of sanity is bright in my head: What am I doing?

He's down on the floor, his victor's stance surrendered. One tiny hand rubs his bottom, the other holds his head. Tears wash his cheeks, his mouth a wide square of sobbing. I don't hear the screaming; my senses have left me and the whole world is silent. I stand now in slow motion, the rod barely balanced on my fingers, the other hand dangling open at my side. I've gone limp, craziness finding its way out the door, leaving me hollow, unable to rationalize any trace of sanity to my behavior.

I am branding this tiny creature with unforgivable memories, scars he'll carry the remainder of his life that will confuse him, switch roles on him, making him—not the hero—but the enemy. Causing him to grow up needing enemies.

There is a terrible ache in my heart over Scott. A fragile string unwinds the memory of a promise wound on some dusty, tangled spool fallen now to the floor in a room I never enter. It says something about healing all my diseases, redeeming my life from the pit, and *crowning me with love and compassion*.

It seems too tangled to be undone.

chapter 13

The Letter

How subtle we think we are at times! I have to smile as I think about the double blessing in realizing we are not. Close friends see the very thing we try to hide. In being found out, we both shatter the crystal of shame and are forced to begin facing ourselves. I'm so grateful for our friends who confronted me about my difficulties—but confronted me lovingly. There are occasions when this insatiable fury still rumbles within my breast. Despite my white knuckles, I'm so afraid it will spill over again someday.

~

One spring evening we visit neighbors a quarter of a mile up the hill from us. The visit over, the night moist with bugs and flying things, Scott begs to walk home with me. Hank climbs into the pickup, his voice full of holding back even as he speaks. "See you when you get home. I'll be waiting."

Since the incline is gradual and I feel younger than I am, I begin to skip—small skips into the descending darkness. Scott is turning into jelly by my side, arms and legs falling limp, crisscrossing each other. He's gone giggly. He can't skip. But he runs along beside me, amazingly well coordinated all of a sudden. In the blackness, I try to put the mechanics of a skip into words. He catches it, tries with both feet, both legs. Jumping awkwardly, then more smoothly, and, at last, he *is* skipping! Skipping in the dark beside me. In unison, we skip. Fireflies twinkle across the field. Somewhere a long, low alarm is going off in insect land; we hear the buzz. And I feel a small, silk-skinned hand slip into mine and squeeze. (How did he find it in the dark?)

I squeeze back slowly. He lowers his little boy voice two decibels. "I just want to make sure I'm still here!"

Why do I remember this delightful memory as clear as the evening it happened?

Months later, during a visit from Hank's mother, she voiced her concern about the way we treated Scott, told us we must change. The command was not enough, however. Didn't she know I'd battled for years to do just that? Deciding to change, wanting it desperately, somehow does not necessarily bring it about!

I felt condemned. The *abused* had become the *abuser!* Automatically. Without my consent. I hated the resentment, yet it stuck to me. It flew in my face. It was out of my control.

After two years of home schooling, Scott has finished the sixth grade and I am through—we enroll him in school. That very summer of 1986 we move to Maryland, where Hank is hired as the director of plant operations for a large nursing home facility. As our routine smooths out I feel a sense of relief, and yet earlier training has made it very clear: Life must not get too good! Too much relief, like an activated bomb, carries an unsuspecting trail of suffering that's often more devastating than the era of misery. No, too much joy or peace is to be feared. What I know is, the dreadful stalks the wonderful, without fail. So, leery of rewards, I pull caution more tightly about me, suspicious of any proffered gift, any remote happiness or success.

Kelly, having graduated from school in British Columbia, now shares an apartment with a friend in Portland. Buff and Scott move East with us. Hank is captured by the new challenges of his work world. Buff is hired by the same facility as Hank, leaving Scott and me together again during after-school hours, vacations, and weekends.

After several months in Maryland, our dear friends, Al and Jan, visit from Washington State. One week under our roof is long enough to see the covert war. They are appalled and speak to me about my attitude toward Scott, now a glaring indictment. It's harder and harder to cover it up. (Surely, the little boy feels the sting of underlying messages, even when I appear better at it than I am. Children always read the underlying codes far better than those portrayed openly.)

"Why do you strive for full control of Scott?" Our friends are disturbed; I'm ashamed. "He is *not* your son. You're *not* his mother. Why do you hold such a death grip on his every move?"

This is the very enigma I can't justify. Their confrontation brings me up short. My strategies turn to powder in the wake of their honesty, unsettling all I do to cope with the dreadful thing. Pretending is useless. Ignoring blatant infractions is not erasing them. The bottom line hits me square on: I am limited. I have unresolved issues. I've been pretending too long, and I've done terrible damage here. Whatever I was afraid of losing is already lost.

It's time to face myself. To face Hank.

I surround myself with the luxury of a fine French café to brave the exposure of my emotional impoverishment. (This is the kind of moment when you realize even at the time that you will remember this. And you do. Forevermore.)

It's an exquisite place. The air offers a moist fragrance upon entering, more than roses, more than baking bread. Tall tapers provide a warm circle of light casting an elongated oval across the eggshell linen tablecloth. A marbleized black bud vase braces up a solitary white bud. In the background, a symphony plays. Strings alive with the pulse of fingertips delicately touch my heartache.

"Just decaf, please." Immersed in a tenseness I've avoided too long, I begin to write, then pause. Waiting for the words to come. It isn't easy to depict in a tracing of black and white the myriad of emotions that strive now for supremacy, that compete to be uppermost, mentioned, remembered by him when the letter is done. My gratefulness. My love for him. My regret.

Cutting away like a surgeon laying back skin, muscle, nerves in neat folds, out of the way, I expose the heart of the matter. It pulsates now before my eyes, astounding me. I can't be who I am not. It's just that simple. My fears, unearthed from beneath some radical nerve, allow the truth to tell itself.

Dear Hank. I can't do the job. He's your baby, not mine. I've tried for seven years to be a mom. I quit.

There is more, much more.

Scott needs you; he's needed you all along. And I need you to take over as parent.

An hour later, the music has changed. Percussion, strength. I ask for a refill and go on.

If you want out of this marriage, I fully understand. I only know I can't go on like this anymore.

Sitting across the dining room table from me, he reads the letter in silence. I work to decipher the message arriving beneath his rolling eyelids. But there's no decoding now. He contains his response beyond me. It hits deep down, touching something that happened a long time ago.

There is little discussion, little to toy with. He stays clear of controversy this time; we both do. I'm barely present myself, completely unsure of the next step.

Then he answers me. No, no, don't leave, he makes it clear. But I fear there is a time allotted for me to deal with this dilemma.

He immediately takes full responsibility for Scott. Naturally, easily, as though he'd been waiting for my letter. I recognize the instinctive, kindred affection fall into place between them once again, reminding me of the boy on the man's lap under a huge white tent with green stripes arching over it one long, hot summer past.

In a strange, empty way I am so relieved.

Twelve-step meetings, therapy, books, I drink it all in. The activity of my hands in making sweatshirts and quilts seems to monitor the craziness of my head, focusing it, venting it toward acceptable outcomes. A type of therapy in itself.

Artwork on clothes absorbs my attention. It's Monday, and I'm into the task of painting a coffee cup on a sage jersey top. The steam rises curvingly to the neckline. The indelible brew simmers now and forever on the left bodice front. Washing colors from the brush in the oval-bottomed sink, seeing the image above it, I can't tear my eyes away. My own image appears strange to me. Why am I busy with the art of these things? What difference does this make to the poverty, the politics, the pathetic hungry children? Colors—light mauve, bronze, black, a dash of violet—being pushed down the drain between my fingers, pressed from sable brush. Pressed and squeezed far longer than is necessary.

The reflection stares back. The reflection of crevices, lines, gullies, faint and deep, revealing how this face folds, has folded for years into agreements, grins, musings, lip bitings, nods. A clear etching of face management, the archaeological study now giving way to patterns acquired more than 40 years ago. An older woman than I know I am returns my stare. Skin turned tissuey, donning a nutmeg age spot as a tribute to the years. But who is she? What will be the description of this life? What will be said of it that's worth remembering?

Perhaps grandchildren will be told, "She was a woman who had a sweatshirt business." "She went to school in her later years and became a 'Woman of Letters.'" A sweatshirt business; a woman of letters! Grandchildren will be told, and grandchildren will forget—and all will be lost by the time it counts. Is there anything else? Anything significant? Has she made at least a simple contribution? How about that one requirement—could the woman love?

That is the question going unanswered.

The woodpile. The recognition of rage beyond control. What is its source, its reason? Am I finally responding to my abusive marriage, or is it something earlier than that? Is it from somewhere in my childhood? my infancy? And why has this intense resentment surfaced since my remarriage? Why does it run full throttle toward Scott? Why *can't* I love him?

chapter 14

The Little Girl

Someone once said, "It takes two lives to live one." No one goes it alone. To grow up healthy each human being needs at least one person who cares unreservedly. It is from that person we learn to care for ourselves. From that one person who is on your side, always available, nurturing. Where was that one person who could, at the critical times, make all the difference? I found her in me.

~

Finally, I'm standing on the grand front porch at this acclaimed place—Caron Institute, recognized internationally as a leader in chemical and co-dependency treatment for almost 40 years. This is the place where people are reported to have undergone spectacular transformations. I feel cynical, tired of waiting. The rain has stopped. The sky has turned plush cerulean, and into it a monarch butterfly traces hoops just above the hedge at the bottom of the stairs. I plunk myself in a rocker and wait for procedures to begin.

At last someone arrives, signs me in, and directs me to the third floor to what will be my room for the week. As I lie flat on the bed I wonder how I went from being an innocent baby to being this enraged woman? What went wrong? Or was I born this way? Coming from a nice family and a supposedly "normal" childhood, what spawned the misery I feel at this moment? Will I get help here? Can it live up to its silly reputation? We'll see, I wager.

On Sunday evening all attendees gather in a large room where we're introduced to each other, to the program, to their ways of priming us for probing our painful pasts. Raised on behavior rather than relationships, we don't grasp how to *do* "relationship." With each new one we lose too much of ourselves.

I wandered through the bookstore after lunch one day in the early part of the week. There were teddy bears and sweatshirts and T-shirts, books all about recovery, and trinkets. One key ring stood out from the rest. It read, "Miracles Do Happen." *Right,* I thought sarcastically. *Not in my lifetime.* Nevertheless, I was drawn to that slogan. I didn't need a key ring—I needed a miracle. I bought the ring, slogan and all, wondering if I would hate the slogan so much by the end of the week that I would throw it away.

My roommate is Pat. She's no more than 25, I would say, and casual from the top of her short brown hair to the clog thongs she stands on. There is a sense about her that she's always in motion. Her silky hair lands to the right side of her head in a breeze, her blouse swings in beside her, her feet pause, ready to go again. She's direct from the start. Introduces herself, wants me to know she's gay, and that she's here to work on her problems. I like her.

We waste no time; we have only five days. Pat's insights are clear. I share with her about Scott, how I fight to be a real mother to him, while I want desperately to send him away.

"Yeah." She smiles. "You need him 6,000 miles away!"

I look at her, puzzled, lifting one eyebrow. "And what does that mean?"

"Don't you feel like you can't protect yourself with him? Wouldn't it be nice to have him 6,000 miles away so you don't have to fend him off at close range?"

I know she gets it. That's *exactly* how I feel!

There are questions to be asked; so many, and so little time. Motivated by desperation, I take advantage of the opportunity and try to plug some new answer into every old question. I meet with my appointed therapist, curious. Richard is younger than I expected. How can he know anything about stepmothering? No more than 30, his baby face surrounded by collar-length, soft curls. His look is

82

pleasant, nicely teethed, eyes the color of lilacs in the sunshine. He has the appearance of being comfortable to hold, is of medium height and build, his light aqua piqué polo hangs to his hips against blue jeans. We sit across one corner of his desk, and I try to pad my way through the differences between us, almost laughing at the absurdity of it all. I could almost be *his* mother!

It doesn't take him long to rescue me, apparently recognizing the difficulty from his own perspective, or by having faced my kind in the past. Before I know it, I'm at ease with him. I ask about manipulation. Without my detailing it all out, he understands what it means to me. It's a way to get a desired response while simultaneously setting myself up—I can never trust what I get.

He guarantees, "The more honest you can be, the less you'll need to resort to the survival strategy of manipulation." His smile takes over his face and contracts a promise.

I remember a banner draped above the blackboard in an old teacher's classroom that read: "Honor is the gift a man gives himself." Right there, at the sound of his words, I purpose to commit to being ultimately honest. No manipulation again, I vow with every fragment of what's left of my integrity. If I don't express my truth, I sacrifice part of myself. Withholding my truth, however small or subtle, deadens me—and I don't want dead anymore.

By Wednesday our sessions become intense. Carving out feelings means sculpting the early family scenario. I'm to set up others from the group to portray my family members, including myself. I carefully survey the room, searching for my mother (or someone who could image her). Their faces look foreign at first, but slowly, as I think about Mom, I point to Marjorie and know she'll do just fine. Weathered beyond her years, probably from overwork, she slumps as if she were boneless, rounded everywhere. Mussed from the day, her tousled hair frizzes around an already sleepy face, yawning now at the thought of playing my mother. (She knows I'm zeroing in on her.) She sits, Indian-fashion, her polyester navies linty from the floor.

Scrutinizing the group again for my father, I spot Ed. At 32, he's slender, with a rough complexion that admits to carrying stress way beyond necessity. His sandy, straight hair persists forward across his brow. Eyelashes lack significance, giving him a colorless look, except for redness rubbed around a squared chin. Of medium height, though he doesn't resemble my father at all in appearance, he bears the familiar knots of anxiety, knots that let me know he's the perfect one.

I set them up, each busy with their own chaos. My father sits with his back toward us all, eyes fixed on the imaginary television set. Nothing, no one, disturbs him. Mom paces wearily, distractedly, from side to side, working, as always, to make it happen. She taps him on the shoulder and calls his name, again and again. He doesn't flinch a whisker. This portrayal is about right. I fight not to be amused.

I scan the room for someone to portray myself and pick a girl named Debbie. She's close to 22, with brown hair longer than her shoulders, parted in the center. Debbie is meek—has been the whole week. Almost invisible. She's medium everything and very quiet. She'll be perfect. She joins the scenario, remaining a specified distance from her parents, and falls to her knees in a corner. She is silently clawing the air, trying to get the attention of Mother, of Father. She grows more and more desperate, but nothing she does works.

And I see her there.

I'm a very little girl. My shoulders droop. I'm already old and bent over with grief. My head hangs down far too low. All I can do is stare at the floor. I'm conscious of the therapists kneeling beside me, a hand on my shoulder, my knee, offering comfort and encouragement to this small girl, all the while helping her to face her reality. Sad as it is, this is how it was for her.

They encourage expression of whatever emotions I'm feeling. I can't contain it any longer, the wailing pushing up from way below emotion. I recognize it as the familiar rumble, undestroyed by all this time. It pushes up and up, forcing its way out through my gritted teeth, despite all the holding back I can muster. Within moments I'm raging in full force—not at my mother or father—but at myself. Wildly pounding the pillows before me, I scream at little me.

"I hate you! I hate you! You should have never been born!" Sweat is pouring from my pores, dampening my shirt. On and on I scream, moaning in between the words. Part of me is shocked that I could hold so much self-hatred. I stay with it, releasing every fraction of the pain into thin air, this air in this room where I feel safe and loved.

Finally, as I face this incredible issue of self-loathing head-on, it breaks into a million pieces, losing its power within me, and I see her for the first time—this little girl as she was then. Defenseless, without a *single* advocate, struggling to join a family barely afloat in its own turbulence. I see her as the full-fledged victim she was then, not the cause of all her parents' issues, but entirely vulnerable to their effects. Emotionally alone in every way, she somehow summoned the courage to continue an uphill battle simply to live. Unable to disclose her agony to another soul, she's held it in, denying its existence, blaming herself for family pain. As accurate emotions emerge, a tremendous sense of compassion arises. Now unleashed sobs are loud and fill with gut-level sorrow pouring out until I'm done. At the end, I am spent. I feel relaxed and open-hearted, like being bathed in the early rains of spring.

The next afternoon we're at it again on the floor in the center of the room. Pillows are stacked all around me. Higher than my head, they stack them. Then on top of my head. I can see only blackness. Their voices are muffled.

"Do you want out?"

"Cindy, do you want to come out? All you have to do is ask." The gentle voice makes it sound so simple. "Just say anything, and you can come out."

It's stuffy under here. Smells like sofas do. Old cotton and body oils. Yet I can't come out. It is *not* simple for me; I *cannot* ask. I can't cry or scream or speak, but quiet my breath instead. Not one sound can escape. Quiet. No sound. Like movie clips displayed in slow motion I encounter myself—unable to ask for help. As a hospitalized infant. Or when beaten by my first husband. Or when having a baby alone. Or any time, ever. Or now, under the pillows. Though I cannot ask directly, unconsciously I'm always asking, yet never able to receive what anyone gives. I want others to *guess* my needs.

As I hover beneath the stacked pillows, the mountain itself seems to box me into the tiny, airless, constricted space—a space where I put myself away many years before. Several minutes later, unable to hold out any longer, I'm uttering a feeble "Help me." Volumes of asking merge together in that weak cry. "Help me, help me." It grows louder and louder. I do want out. Beyond deserving or shame or fear, I *have* to get out!

One by one the pillows topple to the floor as I straighten. The others move in with silent support, gently touching me with their hands, with looks of love. Most significantly, I feel the love I have given to myself in this single act of self-care at a most vulnerable time, risking the admission of my need to another human being.

In this moment I know it's not external factors that keep me bound, but internal ones. *That what I believe about myself is the most damaging—or the most healing—factor of all.*

The week is life-changing, a momentous step in new birth. It has spawned the beginning of self-love. At 43, I'm finding the child within me. Before this special week I didn't know I had one. Now she's vivid in my mind. Too silent for a child, too slow-moving. She has the look in her face of me. Hair the same as I wore mine then, naturally curly hair braided and coming loose. Same body, same low voice. She seems to have a death knell about her. Heavy movements weighted down by something way too big. She wonders if at last she has found me.

Is she a figment of my imagination? Am I concocting her? Surely, she does not live and breathe as I do, yet there remains a part of me in the attic of my mind that holds the child's life intact. Do I dare claim her as mine—or forget this nonsense and go on with life?

The choice is mine. Whether or not to close the door on her and walk away. But I can't do that to her. Not anymore. I relate perfectly to noted author Alice Miller's experience as related in her book, *Pictures of Childhood:* "I made a decision that was to change my life profoundly . . . to put my trust in this nearly autistic being who had survived the isolation of decades" (Bradshaw 1988). Rather than shut the door, I embrace her, a decision that makes a crucial impact on my relationship with myself. I'm cherishing who I am, who God made when He made me.

Leaving this place is difficult. As I hug those around me and gather my bags, I feel a surprising sense of unpolluted hope. Life seems doable—and I'm eager to give it a chance. We wave good-bye, tears flowing freely, hearts more open than any of us could remember. It is just two days before Christmas when I head home.

Evening pours cobalt blue into the canopy above, and single

candles adorn the windows of Amish country, a line of simple stars suspended like a garland hung low over the earth. Old, familiar carols have been fanned to life, their message shooting like luminous sparks into the sweetened air.

"In the manger born a king,/While adoring angels sing."

For the first time in my life I feel "peace on earth and goodwill toward men." Buff has made a lasagna dinner for our returning family that night. Hank and Scott are back from Tennessee, and my mother is visiting with us for the holidays. It will be perfect! I've begun this unique love affair in which the most critical requirement comes *from* me, *to* me! The incredibly foreign notion that I *am* lovable, worthy of my own support and compassion, is the best Christmas gift I've ever received.

I didn't know it, but when Hank left last weekend, he was at the point of ending our marriage. We'd spun around enough. Stalled at a dusty stalemate, with no "next right moves" left to make. No winners, and too much pain.

Our reunion has pivoted us both into optimism.

chapter 15

My Mom

I remember, years ago, kneeling in a puddle by the bathtub one winter evening when Kell had just stepped out to dry off. I was sudsing Buff's washcloth to be sure she was clean all over when her little hand reached out and stopped me. She looked at me straight on as if to say something very important. She said, "Mommy, I don't ever want to grow up." In that moment, Buff capsulized a part of us all. In a sense, we never outgrow the need to be cared for or, to put it another way, we never outgrow the need for our moms. Somehow each of us must absorb enough of our mom's loving care to be able to imitate that to ourselves when the day does come, and we do grow up.

~

Mom . . . Mom . . . Mom." The words form themselves from the hole in my soul like a gaping mouth that utters no sound. Lifting the lid on old emotions releases unbelievable strings of sacred gems, like an old necklace covered with mold and cobwebs. When blown upon briefly, the dust magically lifts, and there in original brilliance is the precious stone. In parenting myself I become aware of the need for my own mom and feel the acute ache of mothering not done. With the intensity of human life held at the moment of death, the agony begins. Agony heard when baby calves, separated from their big cow moms, bawl their loss hard against endless nights.

too hurt to love

As this loss becomes focused I finger the mysterious, maternal jewel (the center pendant), lifting it closer to my eyes and slowly turning it this way and that, scrutinizing each singularly cut edge. I wonder whatever happened to the quality of it. Who robbed Mother of her love?

It's terribly painful, tapping into this innate desire for the first person who ever cared for me at a time when I was the most vulnerable I would ever be. It hurts to know how alone I was then. Before that, a broth of neuroses was kept in check, foaming behaviors hugging the edge of sanity at times. Through established routines of ordinary days that now seem brand-new, certain events, words, situations, trigger the discovery of my grief as I cry out to an adult world, "I want my mom."

Hank has brought a book from Tennessee, one he bought for me as he contemplated the end of our marriage. I'm stunned by the gist of it. Kavanagh's poem (1984) succinctly expresses that universal search and its inevitable culmination:

Who will relieve the sordid thoughts that tear my soul apart,
That leave me exhausted and angry and stretched inside-out
    Like some broken rubber doll?
Who will restore balance and sanity
    when suspicion seems like fact
And insecurity creates its own miasmic world?

Do you not understand that love endures beyond
    the horrors of troubled moments,
    that freedom is the path of love
    and the child must finally
    give up searching for his mother?

In relinquishing this search, I recognize that God assigns my custody to me. But the relinquishing is a "process" (ah, that word that blankets our backslidings with grace and permits us to advance in spite of them). Yes, here at this pivotal point, I must tell you about my mother, who is visiting us now for the holidays. I, having just returned from my week away, my grand unearthing of myself and my developing perspective, truly meet my mom for the first time.

By New Year's Day she has picked up the hint of a foreign fit and begins to investigate. I am a different person. My responses to her have moved out of the old familiar moccasins, bent and twisted into the peculiar shape of her own needs, where I am no longer comfortable.

"What is going on with you? You seem so different." Her voice is whispery, timid to approach the subject.

She sits to my left, the gray-blue upholstery of our recliner seeming to soften the confrontation she enters into. She is silver with middle age, her whiting hair clipped straight and close to her head, her face just slightly pleating into lines around the eyes, the mouth. Her satin cheeks puff like huge pearls, supporting a soft, almost imperceptible fuzz where her sideburns might be. She's short and solidly beginning to round, not obese at all.

"Did I do something wrong?" she asks, her voice fuzzy, decomposing into the inquiry.

For the first time in my life I tell my mom my truth. For the first time in my life I knew it to tell. In taking charge of myself, I'm letting go of the role I've so carefully refined and guarded through the years—that of parenting her. Her face collapses before me, every familiar need trickling into a puddle at her feet, as though I were removing myself from her entirely. Sadness swarms the room and wounds seem to dart back and forth as if enticed forward in time from generations ago. I hear a voice continue and slowly realize it's my own. I am telling her what it was like for me to grow up.

"Mom, you needed too much from me . . . I didn't have it to give. *I* was the child; *I* needed the mom." One by one, I cite instances we both knew in another era, brought forward and registered now to serve their purpose in clarifying the distortion between us.

Several months later in the wash of this meeting, when our exchanges are stumbling along toward something new, I write her a letter to ask for more. Honesty. I'm committed to it now and want it from her. No more double messages, manipulations, false statements about how "I don't mind this or that" when she *is* hurt if I don't guess right. I'm ready to confer my honesty and receive hers.

Two weeks later, Mom telephones me. Her voice is newly stable, gentle. "What do you want me to say?"

too hurt to love

Thinking on my feet in the instant, I tell her, "Mom, I want you to say, 'I know this took a lot of courage for you to tell me these things, and I want you to tell me more.'"

There is a space of silence before she sides with herself. "That's asking a lot."

I side with her, too. "I know it is."

Conversation ends.

In less than 10 minutes she's ringing again. Her voice is low and clear, her own decree eternally decided. "I know this took a lot of courage for you to tell me these things, and I want you to tell me more."

My heart goes soft within me, infant-soft and newborn. "Thank you, Mom. From this moment on I promise to be your daughter fully, telling you what I need from you and my very private truths, even those that claim my difference from you."

Unready to be so vulnerable myself, I promise silently, *Even those truths that proclaim your very existence within me . . . The way I tilt my head like yours . . . The way I file photos quickly against sticky pages of one album after another like you do . . . The way I stand with both feet just 13 inches apart, left hand plunked against left hip . . . The laugh . . . The bend of fingers . . . All like you.*

"I understand, Cyn," she says. "I want you to tell me. I *will* do my best to listen and hear you."

We hang up, and I'm lifted to a dreamy place, all warm and liquid, rocking gently in the darkness. Her response reaches into unused spaces of my heart. Dawdling, as though finding it for the first time, I finger her mother love with rare deliberation. And I'm relieved—she did *not* die under the weight of me.

It would be three years later that my mom delivered, by way of her very presence, another kind of priceless gift. She hadn't visited in almost two years, and I was yearning for her. So during the week of spring break, she and her husband spend a few days with us.

This visit is so different than our others! Typically, when she visits me, I can feel tension start in my head, then gradually spurt through my whole body until every nerve is fraught with anxiety. In fact, I get an infection—the maternal canal disease, triggered by maternal visits.

But this time there is no infection, no tension or anxiety. I feel an uncanny exuberance at the thought of being with her. I'm hailing her arrival as if a queen were coming. In fact, a queen *is* coming!

Ahead of time, I tell her I want to know about her and invite her to share her own life story. Her voice rings grateful for the long-awaited interest in who she is. "I'll look forward to that, honey," she says, and she is suddenly a different person. I sense the privilege that I hold delicately before me.

We meet Saturday evening while the men are watching a baseball game on TV. She sits, warmly pensive in the firelight, both of us sensing the rightness of the hour. This dear human mother, offering me a taste of my own old age, the image of myself in another 20 years—a queen crowned in whiteness, twinkling specks of light toying in her eyes, a mouth trying not to pucker around the lips. She's so tiny! Where did she go as the years flew by?

The windowpane is curtained with a misty gray-blue of old satin; the moon, a circle of light wound together and hung in place. I am eager to not waste a moment with this remarkable woman who, as she relates her own life story, is able to tell me more about myself than I will ever discover on my own.

She sits comfortably, a navy, lintless cardigan gathering on the couch about her seat. Polyester white stretch pants (she's made them herself), lie against her unshaven legs, bare ankles. Softened by several washings, white canvas shoes cross each other and rest in peace. She has a look altogether royal, Italian style, whitened by the years.

"What was it like for you before I was born, Mom?"

Her voice is younger than it was a few moments ago. She speaks easily about herself, storying on about her struggles to raise her siblings alone. An 11-year-old girl, dragged into poverty by the shame of her alcoholic father; an invalid mother.

What were her dreams? her talents? What did she have to bring to motherhood anyway?

She shares the precious visions that prompted her marriage to my father, and speaks of their topsy-turvy wedlock.

Where did all the conflicts go? All the violent screaming of every five o'clock hour, and suppers eaten at the kitchen bar, facing the wall? What did she do with her youth, her visions, then? Into what pocket did she tuck them for safe keeping or future withdrawal?

Some of my questions she couldn't answer. "I hated leaving you and going to work." Her voice drops to the husky undergrowth. "It was the hardest thing I've ever had to do."

I never knew that.

She tells of two miscarriages following my birth.

I never knew about them, either. I didn't know she wanted more children after having me.

She lovingly reminisces about me—the round, rosy cheeks; the dark wad of curls; eyes that blended my father's blue with her dark chestnut, evolving into hazel. She speaks of holding me, missing me, kissing me. She proudly relates how she applied for jobs she knew nothing about, then taught herself skills *after* being hired, without her employers ever realizing she was not trained in the usual way. She reminisces about desperately wanting her class ring of 1941. How, over time, she scrounged out a portion of her weekly wage to buy it, because the bulk of her money went to support her family.

I relish listening to her as she unravels a segment of life that lays the groundwork for my own. It's easy to see her . . . . I recall the brown-and-white photos from the forties, and now set them in action with the stories she's telling. She is young, hopeful, bright, and determined that life will be better than she's known as a child. I finally understand that behavior does not occur in a vacuum—there are reasons we do what we do. For her; for me.

These poignant hours with her enlarge me. I sense a new thing, like a confectioner's light sprinkling of joy on a cool May evening. I see her love in new light—how it's been there for me, on her terms, all along. All along—that last requirement. A human mother with human love. It is enough, after all.

And the unique enmeshment I felt with her—the agony of separation, the resentments and anger—are over. I used to flinch at the sight of my own hands, recognizing how like hers they were. At this moment I examine every finger and knuckle, doting on the similarities.

I sit alone in my rocker and scan the comfort surrounding me. The living room is quiet now, the dying fire projecting only occasional flashes of light into the room. Suddenly I notice, as if for the first time, my revered heirloom—the one heirloom I have left. It is a thumbprint crystal cruet that Mom had given me after my divorce. It had sat in Nana's windowsill for years, lacing the sunbeams pouring into the room with silver ribbons. Nana had given it to Mom herself, and Mom had given it to me when I left New England with my first husband for a new start in California.

I remember standing in the driveway that summer morning. My parents had come to help me pack. With mixed emotions, they realized my need to begin again. But California was so far away, and the finality of it all seemed too intense. My marriage had limped along for years, but moving away to the West Coast was capping off our split with a climactic ending. We lingered by their car a few minutes before they said goodbye. I didn't know when I'd see them again. Their own marriage was in crisis, and we were unsure of so many things then.

Before they left they wanted to give me the thing they'd brought for this goodbye. It was wrapped in tissue paper tucked inside a brown paper bag. "Here, honey, take this with you," Mom said.

Fumbling through the paper, I felt something hard. I recognized the familiar shape of the thumbprint crystal cruet that used to rest on Nana's living room windowsill. Running a finger slowly along its rim, tying up the past in one small circle of affection, I hugged it to my heart. And we said goodbye.

In the process of our divorce, my husband sold my antiques at a flea market in St. Helena, California, to cover expenses. My friend had purchased this treasure from him, rescuing it for me, and returned it during our visit to her home a few years before. Her thoughtfulness reflected an enormous gift—in returning that cruet she had returned a part of myself. It rests on my windowsill today. In the firelight the aurora of its prism sides throws dancing colors on a quiet wall across the room and remind me of God's regard for the tiniest of treasures. I am keenly aware of and deeply touched by the threads of soft gold running through my life.

chapter 16

A Dream

Can you recall specific messages you've received from God? Does He repeatedly communicate to you in specific ways? I find that He has a very personal way of doing this with me—He uses timing. His timing increases the impact of His message to awesome proportions, enhancing the minutest detail with astounding import. The following dream is etched in my memory as one of those crucially timed E-mails, creating virtual reality for me.

~

Mom's deliverance encourages my stepping up before the throne of God with the truth of who I really am. Restraining my emotions on behalf of the God I knew—a God without them—I cautiously presume to unload all I dare to at His marvelous pierced feet. I feel incredibly ashamed. Ashamed of my very being. But I struggle through old admonitions and begin the confession. Feelings buried a long time ago rise to the surface and circle with mounting fury, swirling now in a frenzy to which I must surrender. Spinning into a blur, rigid episodes of admonishment, of cut-and-dried performances, and merciless words pounded into podiums of the past, all add to the hysteria of the moment.

"I hate what You made. I hate You for making me the way I am." Before His awful presence I'm still standing! "You're mean to make me so bad, then require me to be perfect. Why *this* life for me? Why so late in making any difference? Why can't I quit hating Scott? What's wrong with me?"

Questions I've lugged around for years spill all over His majestic lap. To my absolute astonishment He does *not* kill me—or even punish me for this outrage. Instead, I feel myself wrapped ever so gently into a divine embrace, the kind that takes in all my past and all my future, gripping the present tightly between us. I'm lifted like an infant bird held in the palms of an old man's hands, safe and tender and steady. He holds me. Then, slowly, the strange skirmish subsides. The fight loses its footing, and I'm done. Absolutely calm. Settled. Alive. With the awesomeness of a child watching her first golden sunrise I lay hold of a profound truth: All the things I ever thought about God are not true. And all the things I never dared dream about God *are* true. It is a private revolution.

Historically, religion had held its own kind of clout for me, irrefutably validating childhood claims that God *was* beyond my reach, that self-love *was* the worst sin of all. In traditional reverence I always began my prayers with "Dear God . . ."

One night Hank questioned me about that formality. "Why not, 'Dear Father'?" he asked.

Such an endearment was not a term I associated with God. Nevertheless, his question bothered me. I lay awake, wondering about how God did think of me, if at all. That very night I had a dream. It was a lifelike dream with all the vividness of three-dimensional impact—colors, scents, and sounds . . .

I'm 23, and holding my second infant daughter. She faces me as her weight settles on my forearm and against my chest. The softness of her cheek rubs against my own. I smell her babyness, a mixture of powder and brand-new skin. She is more than beautiful!

I hold an ocean within my heart for her. I love her so much. I can't seem to get close enough, long enough. I'm awed by her. She does *nothing* wrong! In her very being is pristine joy itself. During afternoon naps I wait outside her room, sometimes in it, missing her. In church, when she giggles right out loud, I can't hold back my own. Dirty diapers marvelously provide playtime again. They're no bother at all. When she topples a vase to the floor and it shatters into a million pieces, it's *really* all right. The broken thing means nothing to me. Fresh mother love fills me to the brim, spilling over into her development, her recognitions. It's a lively, lovely connection we have. I cherish it, adore her, and relish the dream time.

Waking up from my dream places that time out of reach—too far to go back to embrace again. She's grown now. A woman in her own right. Baby days are over, and I can't pull myself together. Grieving her baby loss, I crave that time again. I wish I could hold her in my arms, catch her scent, feel her velvet skin against my cheek. Love spills out on my damp pillow in longing for what is over.

As I recover that morning, new glints of revelation sprinkle down from the sky and land at my feet. I begin to understand that in giving me the dream, God wants to wake me up: *He loves me!* I see that sin is simply separation from God. It's when, after all, I don't believe His love, when I don't love myself or others. The dream brings into microscopic view the panorama of divinity—a Parent in love, enraptured with His beloved child, like I was in my dream. The zealot for us, radically devoted to all that we are. Unequivocally cherishing! Yearning for us while we sleep, savoring the feel of us in His arms. His utter delight exists in our joy. He's ardent, compassionate in tending to our humanness. Our mistakes are wiped clean as though they never happened. With passion fresh every day, He loves me!

And I find it worth considering anew who He is—a world Creator, a timeless Spirit, a Gift giver beyond all gifts ever given. His is the heart that impeccably wraps me in grace! I'm perfectly loved as intimately as *this* God can love. He celebrates *who* I am. My thoughts swirl around in my head, clearing out a stockpile of doubts in one sweep. Why hadn't I seen this before? Was I afraid to be this loved? To trust it? It sounded too easy.

In reading Scripture in the past, like a magnet to the pole, I extracted every rigid rule with its impossible requirements, and each one perpetuated my beliefs in a harsh, stern God and a defective me. But this message is different; now I matter! Distinctly opposite verses leap from the page. *You will forget the shame of your youth. You are precious, honored, loved. I love you better than you know. Nothing can ever change that fact.*

"*Is* it a sin, Father, for me to love myself?"

He had spoken gently through my dream this night and said,

"No, sweetheart. This is how I love you. This is how you can love yourself and how you can love other people, too."

I finally decide that if I'm to lose heaven because of loving myself, then I will lose heaven. If heaven means going back to the 40 years I spent in self-loathing, then heaven *is* hell. Weary of manufactured love, I give up the production. I just want to love myself and begin to love God. "If this is not OK with You, help me with it. My love is so distorted that I don't think I know how to really love others. And myself, not at all. Just let me take in Your love for me so Your love is what comes out."

The "nurture/nurture" principle is grasped at last—nurture myself, so that I can nurture others!

chapter 17

Confrontation

Wouldn't it be marvelous if our issues could be gone in the twinkling of an eye? Then my story could have ended here with a finale of resolutions bursting like fireworks into the night sky.

But that's not what happened.

As the years passed, the bond between Hank and me grew stronger in some ways, but there remained a constant living ache between us. However, tiny seeds of healing had been planted.

≈

I begin sifting through the religious rules of my past, discarding the prehistoric and obsolete, while elaborating on freshly picked insights. This act of sifting and sorting proves to be one of the most important pieces of all in shifting my perspective. Although my struggle to truly love Scott continues, from this point on, a very different attitude gradually edges its way into place. And I slowly begin to realize that the first experiences of "crowning with compassion" must begin with me: I view myself with compassion *even* as I continue to fail.

The morning is newborn, each blade of grass tipped with tiny cubic zirconias, waiting for the sun to scoop them away. Trees are thickly green overhead, clapping their hands together in the old paper-rock-scissors game. I wonder who comes out on top? To the east, a deer runs out of my vision and into the first glimmer of sunlight. Our arms lock together in place as Hank and I pass the familiar landscape on a quick-paced walk.

"I love it when you smile like that and I don't know what you mean." Hank's grin lurches across my thoughts. We're discovering the limits of our intimacy, where fences disappear altogether, and we risk oneness for a while. Then, suddenly smacking up against the highest fence (perhaps he remembers Scott), he emotionally turns full tilt around, his back to me, carrying on almost as if we have never met. Bracing into a dusky, mauvey, shadowed movement of some other purpose, he finds a side of himself that steadies without me. And we're apart again.

Quiet now, and still walking. My own thoughts circle back where again I dream of my life without this monstrous resentment. What would it be like to freely and largely love Scott without this hatred grinding away at my responses, my pseudo-mothering of him?

"Don't jam yourself up, needing to make him wrong." I can almost hear Hank's thinking about Scott as loud as his voice might be. All my dark concerns with performance, with hard-core duties and diligence, seem to be flaking off; an airy, baby-blue ease moving in, lighting up my world, freeing it from the striving toward perfection. Yet the ongoing argument persists in my head, opposing forces vying for supremacy. *If I* were *a Christian, if I* were *truly healing, I would be loving Scott.* And then: *But why does he have to be here? What about his own mom?*

I don't need to tell you how weary we all get of this thing, this thing driven by a very dull, very old issue. What issue is it? And what about that necessary requirement I couldn't tag for Jeannette, the one my someday-husband must have, the name of it on the tip of my tongue yet refusing to come to mind. That issue, this issue— they are the *same* issue! That nebulous issue is the issue of *unconditional love!*

Hank's profile always attracts me. All rosy-fleshed from brisk walking, it's carved beautifully now against the edge of morning, his silvering hair waving away from his face. I work diligently to redistribute my excesses—behaviors and beliefs from one area to another, discarding most, retrieving others, and coming into balance myself.

In momentum with our stride, my thoughts shift. I ponder aloud the origin of the mundane. "Who gave the directions their names—north, south, east, west—do you know?"

Hank chuckles. "I haven't learned that one yet, but you do know that is 'NEWS,' don't you?"

It takes me a moment. "No kidding!" (I really didn't know.)

"Yeah, that's where it comes from, and it looks like you've been left out in the cold again," he says with a half-laugh.

Several minutes pass before our turnaround point. I'll get him back. "When you reach into a bag of jelly beans, do you take the orange ones first because you like them least? Or do you take the licorice because they're your favorite?"

He doesn't answer, just grins to my eye, letting my quizzy thoughts roll around inside awhile before even bothering to sort them out. We're quiet on the way back, but within me echoes another question I'm not sure ever forms on my lips: "Do you have any idea how good you are to me?"

Mornings later on the trail of this worship hour, I'm jolted awake by almost a nibble of pain at my consciousness. I remember that it's June. This Monday morning Hank has just left for work, Scott's gone to school, and all is quiet. No sleepy elevator music. Nothing. Just the ceiling fan humming unevenly above the commotion below. After wiping the sink, the counters, the stove—anywhere I thought *he* had been—I put the Cheerios away and sweep the floor. My perpetual anxiety is escalating. I dread the approach of summer, resist its sunbeams stretching prematurely across kitchen walls.

It's been three years since I first discovered myself and my reality. I have faced Mom. Faced God. There *are* changes. My compulsivity, for instance. Daily our bed is unmade and dust accumulates on night tables and picture frames. I step over dirty laundry. I laugh harder and cry less. Fuming at passing motorists is down to the bare minimum—only when I'm hungry. Something like a tightly woven bud is flourishing inside, a bud that unfolds in the presence of challenge and sends off the feeling of competence to every nerve and tissue, declaring, "I *am* intact! I *am* able to meet the thing before me."

But in spite of growth and healing, my resentment is growing bigger, just as Scott grows bigger. And summer means Scott and me together again. I feel the sting of our situation. Blended, we are not. And being stuck flattens life out to one dimension, like a stepped-on egg.

Why couldn't Scott visit his own mother this summer? Why couldn't he go to school there in California? For some reason, I've never said this before, never confronted Hank about sending Scott West. Under his generous authority my compulsion has always been for Scott to stay with us. I'd refused to relinquish my chances with him, to give up. I believed there would come a day (I dreamed of it) when I would rally with new energy, my positive thinking coming to life under the magic of overuse, much like the velveteen rabbit. I imagined my mechanical parts filling with human blood that coursed through my arms and feet, my head, my heart. And then I would be able to love him profusely. But this is not happening. Right now, as healed as I am, all I can do is demand he go away.

"We need to talk," I offer, labeling *my* need under the guise of "we."

He sits in his recliner with bare feet suspended on the leg lift, Big Dog T-shirt and well-worn Wranglers all working with him to look relaxed. My voice is a taut rubber band, so I try compensating, deliberately flexing the intonations in marshaled optimism.

"I want to talk to you about Scott."

He braces himself.

I pump what I think is courage from the point I have substantiated in my head. "I've put in 10 years with Scott. He's not a little boy anymore." My voice sounds like someone else's; whose, I don't know.

Moving on, I submit what seems at the time to be a reasonable option. "Let him spend the summer with his own mother. Why couldn't we give it a try?"

He doesn't blink an eye, just keeps looking right through me. I think how like him this is not to lower his defense yet.

"The way it is with us, it's not good for Scott to keep him with me anyway. I didn't deserve it; neither did he."

No resistance is forthcoming, so I drop the ultimatum at his feet. My voice is strong now, sure. As sure as I've been about anything in my life. "If you don't send Scott out there, I'm leaving. I can't do this anymore. Think about it for the next few days and let me know."

Three wordless days later Hank breaks the silence. "Let's talk." There's a vague tragedy in his voice. I don't like it. Back in the den, almost horizontal in the recliner now, eyes mere slits as though watching a baseball game, he gathers all the relaxation he can bring to the moment. "I just can't kick him out. I want him to be able to stay at least until he's 18. I was 14 when I left home, and there was nowhere for me to go. But I knew I couldn't stay. It was awful. A 14-year-old boy shouldn't have a death wish. It's too much to ask of me to do that to Scott. I couldn't live with myself if I did."

He says this for the first time, but I already knew. His commitment sinks gravely onto my courage, my hope. The oppression settles in more densely than ever.

Looking me in the eyes, he leans forward with both feet on the floor now. The recliner doesn't relax him anymore. "But I don't want you to go either. I don't know what to do. I don't have an answer for this. If you have to leave, I understand, but I can't abandon him like I was abandoned."

It's over. I need to walk.

Occasional fireflies already skip through the blackness, blinking, flashing here and there. Trees hulked against the night sky fill in the emptiness, and a peeper chorus chants its way into summertime. Honeysuckle pours its sweet fragrance across the meadow where I know black cows are standing in a black night. As though a grenade has veered its way directly into my brain and blown it to smithereens, I feel fragments flapping around the crater in my mind like many thin, gray rubbery leaves banging against the wind, each with their own disconnected thought.

One leaf: *Yes, yes. Huddled together, mother and I, from birth. From this place I plot my approach to the world.*

Another leaf: *A first husband—fury in slow motion, muscles distended, shoulders moving beyond time with a force to beat hell itself into place. Slow motion, close to graceful, ordering the next blow as by committee arrangement. I'm unable to break loose.*

Another: *How he has grown! The tiny wisp of a boy now nearly a man. Oh, God! I've missed my chance to love him!*

Another: *The cries of hatred toward myself unearthed during my week at Caron—and the cries of hatred toward Scott, buried for years—they are the same cries . . .*

too hurt to love

Hank's "No" tossed the choice back to me. If I left, I felt as though I would lose altogether. If I stayed, I would have to continue in this struggle to love Scott. It's hard to fight for something when you don't know what the thing is you're fighting for. Nevertheless, I withdrew my ultimatum. I was not ready to give up the search for more pieces of myself.

～

Walking . . . What would I do without walking? The steps themselves bring a centering. I feel thoughts come to order around the table; the gavel hits against rationality. Awareness of our differences shoots through me. I need to be more like Hank; he completes me, a perfect complement.

Walking steadily, pounding the earth now with the imprint of each step.

Who is Hank, this man I live with? To me, he is the embodiment of all that is manhood. I see the picture clearly: his broad, strapping shoulders, hoisting with a synchronized ease, stacking 100-pound cartons of books as if he were lining up hat boxes on a milliner's shelf, deliberate, steady. His deep brush of a voice, his robust spirit, the grounded set of his body bearing a surprisingly smooth precision. I can't begin to tell you the spin he can put on a ski boat, or his polished suspicion of looming social programs, or promises of tax relief. Even his preference for consequential punishment and payback and earning one's own way, as opposed to handouts—all components of the abused boy grown to be a man.

How easy it is to forget, in his blustering about, his grand capacity for tenderness, that fine point wedging far below the everyday clamor of manliness—a delicate sensitivity to precious things. There's a secret part that responds in perfect accord to unspoken cues, a synchrony of my soul with his. He stands strong against the backdrop of a coral sunset, yet so at the lip of things—vulnerable, willing, trusting. What an absolute treasure lies within my grasp! I consciously and deliberately brush up against loss of him in my mind, attempting to dilute the impact for the day when it might land at my feet.

chapter 18

Hidden Giant Steps

Slowly, life as I knew it began to lighten up. As if someone poured color into a black-and-white world. Or suddenly tipped the incline I'd been trudging uphill onto a horizontal plane. I felt new ease flow into my days—and dreams of my own began to crystallize.

~

More pieces of myself are gradually redeemed.

I stayed too long in my imaginary prison—that constricted cubicle of beliefs about myself and my own personal history. From this single perspective I defiled every future relationship for too many precious years, not knowing the war had ended decades before. Not knowing that often today's battle is redundant, futile. For the already grown-up, childhood foes can no longer be beaten down—not really. Victories are for current struggles. It's well to know which is which. And the blessings . . . I am drawn to recognize the blessings.

Pops, my father, is one of those blessings. He calls on Sundays. Every Sunday of my life, nailing down his love at 9:00 a.m., ready or not. Whether I'm awake or asleep, he rings and assures me of who he is and of his love for me. His handyman stories of elderly neighbors who need his help, his grass-cutting skills, his remote-control fixing, his answering machine setting, his porch step repairings. The conversation bursts prematurely open, like a furry dandelion globe caught by a surprise wind. He throws out ideas, opinions, handles for me to latch on to and agree with.

But my thoughts glide above the issue at hand and around it, hoisted out of reach by my own concerns for him, unspoken worries about his underlying messages, his loneliness, his ability to cope with aging; then back to the matter we attempt to solve right here on the spot. This conversation lands unsynchronized, exploding at my feet. Yet, Sunday mornings would fall out of line if Pops didn't call and tack his love up on all four corners to the old bulletin board that leans against the sunlit side of my heart. A worn advertisement, yet well read, well attended, of that unnamed requirement he does so well.

In moments like these the afterglow reaches higher proportions. That sweet effect of overall goodwill, the essence of well-being turning all divine—where everyone is good and everything is fine. The sweet, sweet ambience brought on by a brisk walk, a money gift, a phone call from a lost friend, an accomplishment—or a phone call from my Pops.

~

Through our years together I have found myself molding to Hank's style of living. Regardless of my tendency to lodge into a familiar groove, his spontaneity derails the expected and enlarges me. I feel quite sure that I have yet to understand the value of all this in the global assessment of my life. However, one insight is clear: the rewards of commitment are not saved for the end. The tastes of unconditional love along the way are the real prizes. And Hank has given me these in his "random acts of kindness," when I was least looking for it.

"Lou! Lou, what are we doing tonight?" The house warms under the glow of his entrance and we make a plan. A country drive. A walk. A frozen yogurt. A video. I look for this daily Christmas packaged in allotted time. Hank animates my world, expands me, makes me laugh in the middle of the night. Where do the bright and ruffled streamers come from in my ordinary days? He gifts me with himself in ways I least expect. One day this came packaged at my feet.

It is April 9, and I'm reading at our dining room table. He plows through the door and stands there, dressed in better-than-work clothes, shopping bags hanging from both hands.

"Where have you been?" I'm dumbfounded.

"I've been shopping!" he announces with satisfaction.

My surprise is evident, confusion still clearing a space for me in the scene at hand.

He puts his bags down and pulls out several silver boxes, wrapped in huge bows of red and pink, and sets them on the table. Surprise rides all over his face. I'm not sure if it's his, or a reflection of mine. "Open them, Lou."

Stunned, and stalling for time, I demand, "What's going on here?"

Undeterred, he presses, "Come on, just open them."

I slowly slide one of the silver wrappers off and lift the tissue paper, feeling my throat parch instantly. I don't get it. How can I have all this? And why?

Inside lies a pink coat dress that fits me perfectly. Another box reveals a navy-and-white three-piece suit. There are accessories to match, and shoes and hose all coordinated together. Every item is exquisite, beautiful. Dazed by the bounty, I turn to him. "What is this for?"

His face is absolutely aglow with the giving. His eyes almost squeezing back the joy. "It's my birthday!"

His side-job money, his creativity, his love, bought us the moment. It is the day before *his* birthday!

In an instant, I *do* get it. His giving overwhelms me. I put both my arms around his neck, hanging on, catching another glimpse of the gift he is. I know it's time to stop rejecting the good things.

≈

February 1990. Al and Jan phone (the friends from Washington State who once confronted me about my treatment of Scott). Excitedly, they chime in together, "We have a plan, and it can't wait!" It's Jan's birthday, and her one request is to go to Hawaii *with us*. "Do you want to go?"

Hank and I, on different phones in the same room, respond, "Absolutely!"

This definitely does not fit any expectations I've ever had for myself. In fact, this offer soars above any goals I have. I couldn't see myself in any such role. To do certain things, empowered things, seems beyond the me I know. There are places I've never dreamed of going; there are roles I've never dreamed of playing. They do not match my earlier postures or predicaments—the ill infant, the beaten wife. Although now my perspective is modified, my grasp on reality is firmer, and my energies are targeting growth, my feet seem bound in the concrete grave of the oppressed.

In spite of all this, we board the plane, heading for Oahu and Maui. On beaches like white crystal, spread wide under postcard blue skies, we experience Hawaii. Chartreuse, fuchsia, and orange parrots induce doubts that this can be real. It is truly awesome! I *can* go places I never dreamed I'd ever go, and reach goals I never dreamed I'd reach.

Back from Hawaii, as I'm mopping the kitchen floor, I become strangely aware of the changes within me. Certain ideas take shape with each slap of the mop, seeming to wipe away muddied places on the floor of my mind. My commitment is that nothing I do will cater to my illness. This process of change has been arduous and exhausting at times, yet it's been a breeze compared to what life would be without it. Newly attuned to the present, old inner movies subside, misbeliefs, evaporate. I have a surplus of energy now bubbling up, ready for new directions.

Freer than I've ever felt, I careen around bends in my experience, discovering the art of simply "being." What I used to think was lazy behavior I now realize is vital play, how a child learns to live in the world. Today I relish the sacred times when I can porch-sit spring evenings away, dishes waiting until the last embrace of sunset disappears. I'm lured by the flaming fingertips of daylight behind the horizon. Priorities find new time pockets, altogether fresh values. Even the notion I must have a working plan to relax seems futile.

The newness is pervasive. Struggling with one issue, while hanging on to new insights, I discover that effects multiply, and healing ripples out beyond the conscious sore spots. Amazingly, improvement spreads to unsuspecting parts, just as the pain has done.

I'm still mopping. I'm not sure, but I think I remember peeling the plastic off a piece of cheese, folding it in half—the American white cracking in two as it bends—and popping it in one bite into my mouth.

I begin to scrutinize my wildest dreams. The Hawaii trip has opened to me the impossible ones. Not the dwarfed ones, trimmed down just so to fit possibility. Not those obliged to surrender to the terror of the moment. No! The vast, expansive, glorious, beyond-containment dreams.

Though my business flourishes, a discontentment is gradually developing. I want more. I want to work with people, with those who travel life mechanically, lured toward attachment with other human beings, but with the fits and starts of a dying engine, they achieve only a silhouette of relationships with others and, undoubtedly, no hint of even that with themselves.

The next morning, lingering longer than I need to in the bathroom, I sit on the edge of the tub. Hank's shaving. I watch him soap his face, cleaning away his heavy beard with a few practiced sweeps of the razor. The words form themselves, casually, one after the other, and stumble out into his shaving lather.

"I think I'd like to go to college," I say.

He freezes a moment, then lowers his half-shaved face into mine. "You can do it. If I did it, you can too." He'd completed college two years before while working full-time. I honored his accomplishment, never considering it for myself. He's positive it will be a breeze. "Get a schedule. Pick a course you'd like. Give it a try."

This seems like the next right thing. I register at Montgomery College for a speech class the following week.

That May, walking onto the campus as a 46-year-old, I feel like a 6-year-old on my first day of school. I can hardly contain myself! There's enough money from the sale of my business to pay for my entire college education, including a master's degree. It's a gift of grace that says, "Go for it!" A warm car waiting for me at 6:45 on dark winter mornings, a hot drink in a travel mug, and a packed lunch—I read all of them by heart as another "go ahead" from Hank.

Learning becomes sweeter through years of practice as my stale cognition sparks with discoveries. I find ways to stomp out the remains of self-doubt left flickering in the dregs of battle. At last I graduate with a bachelor's degree in social work, magna cum laude—which staggers my senses. The next year I obtain my master's, then pass the state board licensing exam, validating my professional work. I continue to honor with gratefulness how carefully God has led me all along to do the very work I now do.

Nevertheless, my progress was suspect to my family, despite the giant steps I knew I'd taken. Unfortunately, they were the kind of giant steps that didn't always show. Unfortunately, the things left undone appeared all the more grotesque in the face of improvements.

chapter 19

The Third Birth

Outside our bedroom window tree branches jostle in the wind, and snow crystals dance atop a fresh covering. Another morning crowns the day with possibility. Today is alive with intense brightness, yet I still carry pieces of the ugly broken monster. Those pieces must go.

~

It is late February 1993. Bryant Gumbel's voice filters through to the kitchen, muffling today's news. Putting away supper dishes preserves me in the mundane. Hank is reclining in the old blue recliner in the den. Leaning over the kitchen sink eating a succulent orange, Scott mutters something, between dripping its juice into the sink, about money from Dad. My ears perk up.

I'm certainly not aware of any such money. We usually share that kind of decision, bouncing it off each other for input. The familiar curl tightens in my stomach. Hank obviously didn't want me to know about this. *Wait, wait,* I think. *Take your time; think it through. There must be a reason.* But I'm barely listening to myself.

"What money?" I grill Scott, squeezing civility from the warnings in my head.

"Oh, some of it is the money he gave me last week."

Last week? *Last week!* What kind of unity have we here? The question roars into the fire, uprooting all belief in him.

too hurt to love

While Scott lingers with the orange drippings, I head for the blue recliner. "Can I talk to you?" I ask between gritted teeth.

We head upstairs to our bedroom and close the door. I know I'm bent forward at the waist, yanked there by the curling stomach tension. My face is screwing into a rage and reddening before him.

"What about this money to Scott, and why didn't you tell me?"

He refuses to succumb, the calmness in his voice smoother than ever, caretaking me. "I just didn't want you to be upset. I didn't want to argue about it. So I just gave him some money."

"This does not work for me!" Louder, with the hard hit of betrayal. "At this point in our lives, if we can't be honest, I don't want any of it. I don't do this anymore, not in life, not in marriage, not anywhere." The ultimate ultimatum is reached. I am truly done with this, all of it. Nothing left to fight with, or for.

Hank is not up to it either. He turns around without flinching, opens the door, and descends to the stuffed recliner. Back to Bryant Gumbel, back to the news of the day. How he does this is beyond me.

Silence piles thickly around us, one silence stacked on top of another, like cumulus clouds painted in angel pictures. For days the only mentionable things are the necessary ones. Any serious discussions are impossible, impossible to either hear or speak.

Exhausted with each other, with the horrible weight of absence, three nights later we attend a five o'clock movie. Popcorn doesn't do it, so after the movie I suggest french fries and coffee (foods I touch only in extremes). We pull into a fast-food store, and one large fry, two decafs later, Hank proposes we take a drive and heads for Gold Mine Road.

Gold Mine is washed in watercolor golds and violets of evening rain, the backs of leaves glistening wet overhead, hanging low above the roof of our pickup. Cloistered between drenched trees, we follow the curve of the braided road, strewn with fallen branches, some the size of logs. The soft, steady step of raindrops across the roof washes beauty down side windows. We drive along, knowing the time has come, just waiting for the space to begin.

Hesitantly at first, I hear him break the spell, his voice soft upon entering. "I love Scott so much." He backs off, then begins over again. "I want to give him so many things, but I never feel like I can."

It's the first time I've heard this from him. I turn my head to see the full confession and find his face breaking apart. Fighting for control, he freezes the breakage into place, tears a complete wash across his cheeks. "I love you now and I always loved you, no matter what you felt for Scott. I love you for just you. I know your limitations; I don't care about that. It just hurts me so much to know you don't like my boy." Gulping tiny breaths between words, he keeps going.

"I just wish it were different." His broken heart is being delivered all over the front seat. "I wish I could change things, but nothing I do makes any difference. I just don't want to lose either one of you. And this is awful. I don't know what to do."

I fight against shock, trying to grasp what I'm hearing. From the beginning I believed Hank's love for me was dependent on my performance, particularly I knew it rested on how I loved his son. I believed he couldn't love me any more than I could love Scott. It seemed the risk of loving was just too great. Yet here he is, loving anyway. Loving Scott like I always knew he did. Loving me almost more than I dare realize.

I hear his love, his pain, his commitment, pouring out in spite of his resolutions. Something is happening to me, something extremely significant, something unlabeled. A thick skin is being ripped from my heart as I hear my husband rip open his own. Intercourse of the heart—that unattainable union, after 12 searching, agonizing years, unfolds right into our hands. All the experiences of the past years merge together in clarity, stipulating self-love, God's love—and now Hank's love. Sifting slowly into consciousness is the splendid power of unconditional love.

The cruel boulder that threatened our destruction now dislodges. It moves, rolls, tumbles over the edge of the cliff, gaining momentum as it plunges into the depths below. With it goes every resentment I've ever felt toward Scott during the past 12 years, that surfaced every moment of every day. That made me cringe inside when I knew he was home, or that he had touched certain food, or clothes, or *anything*. That shameful hatred we had all lived with for too long—that threatened to destroy even the changes—all melts away in this moment. I'm struck still, unable to respond.

"I hear you. I hear you, Hank." That was all I could say.

I slide between the sheets that night, afraid to believe the reality of what has happened to me. Surely, the next morning I will feel the same familiar rancor. Surely, I will lose this sweet, sweet peace. But the next morning is unlike other mornings. I awake engulfed with a rush of something miraculous. The resentment is gone! I am truly free! I keep this miracle to myself, afraid it will end if I articulate it, like a mirage that disappears when you try to touch it. But as the next day comes and goes, I feel even greater freedom, carrying this milestone like a fragile heirloom, yet bursting with its value. Two days later I confess it to Hank. My mouth forms the words without emitting sound at first; sound stuck in my throat somewhere.

Finally: "Something's different, Hank, very different. I'm not resenting Scott at all, and I'm not even trying not to." My voice chokes with tears, and I'm sobbing. "I'm not only *not* resenting him, I'm *loving* him, loving him so much my heart is breaking for him."

Now I can't stop, rolling over the cuff of my heart, spilling its contents into a land that has waited too long to receive it.

"Something terrible is over, ever since our talk the other night, and I've been so afraid to believe it." Shivers shoot up my spine at the idea of it all being just a dream. It *must not* be just a dream. "Although I don't know for how long, I know it's not a part of me anymore."

I feel Hank's arms around me, holding me as close as we can get, for a very long time while we both stand very still, caught in the oddly silent, invisibly edged, eye of a miracle.

I ask God to keep the resentment away while continuing to affirm how much He loves me, how *I* love me. And slowly, gradually, love for Scott floods me, coming like a river whose dam has broken, bursting, rushing, pushing aside everything in its path. I have all I can do to wait for him. I sit motionless in my room that afternoon, deeply cherishing new dimensions of motherhood, those chips of precious jewels lost to him, lost to me. Now the remains, the broken chips, are selected from floor sweepings for redeeming the time lost.

I know Scott's footsteps will soon echo up the stairwell, as they have for so many days and years before. How I had dreaded that sound! But today my heart waits to hear the familiar slam of the back door and his lanky body bounding up the stairs to his room, where he's learned to go directly. Now time seems to slow almost in reverence while my heart races. Waiting today is very different. The air itself is charged with my anticipation. I hold my breath, listening. I *want* to hear his steps, his voice. I *want* him to come home!

At last the car pulls into the gravel driveway. I wait. A few moments later the kitchen door slams shut. Seconds pass, but Scott doesn't bound upstairs as usual. For some reason, his steps are slow and deliberate, yet steady. As he approaches the landing I'm there to meet him, and we look at each other carefully. He knows I'm different before the words come. Just by looking, he knows. There are no words for the moment. Tears are streaming down my cheeks. Really looking him in the eyes for the very first time, I notice how like his Dad he is, how unspeakably precious he is. The silence is brimming with unspoken things.

Somehow I must find words. "Scott, you know it's over, don't you?"

He stares back at me, then nods his head in a slow yes.

Hesitatingly, I reach my arms out to hug him, and he lets me. A vibrant life force flows through me to him unlike anything I've ever experienced before as I hold this young man who for 12 long years I could not mother. And I know from this moment on that he is *my* son.

"Can I take you with me today?"

His nod tells me he wants to go. We leave in late afternoon, heading for the mall. I want to buy him the world. We enter a café and take our seats at a quiet corner table, candlelight cutting a bubble around us. I'm not sure how to enter the world of the young man before me. His boyish face brims with manhood, a dabble of whiskers fringing his chin. Those hazel eyes sort out years of confusion, of blame and abuse he didn't deserve. It would be easier to run away, but his whole being draws me in closer.

He gives his order to the waiter. He knows what he wants. I ask for a Caesar salad and decaf, wondering if this whole scene is really real.

During dinner we crack the silence of too many years. Feeling more grateful than ashamed, the words gather themselves deeply from my heart. "Scott, I am so sorry. I know that my words may fall like rain on your heartache, but you must hear this truth at least: None of this was *ever* your fault. Not for a single moment did it *ever* have anything to do with you. It was always, always about me and my inadequacies."

He matches my stare, the color of my eyes, with his own.

"I would give my life to have had it different for you."

Not a muscle twitches as he leans forward, both elbows spread wide under his leaning. His expression drinks in my words, the dabble of whiskers quivering now in belief.

Tears brim over and garble my speech. "It's been a long and terrible journey, but at last I've found a way to love myself. And in doing so I've discovered how much I love you."

The sobbing party of two takes a break to collect ourselves.

"What's it been like for you, Scott?" I ask, inviting his agony into my heart.

And he begins to tell me. Our talk winds into evening, beginning to connect us in ways we had missed all those years. Later, when we have exhausted ourselves, we try a bit of shopping, deciding colors, styles, sizes. On and on, with deliberateness, I am discovering him. I want to know all there is. At last we head home, content for the time being, in the place we've found with each other. A place we both needed so long ago.

~

This miracle happened in early 1993, and my love for Scott continues to grow deeper. Many sharing times have followed since that rainy day ride with Hank, times filled with an unspeakable ache for what could not be, yet holding unspeakable joy at finding, as my own, my most precious son.

There is no making up to Scott for what I was unable to do. Nothing is enough—not apologies, not admission of my limitations, not promises. What could I ever do that would make up to him the years I could not love? I only know that I am a different person filled with loving him. I am no longer a victim, no longer a perpetrator.

I remain awed by the truth of it all. How does it happen? Piece by piece, day by day, prayer by prayer, love act by love act. When the last requirement of love breaks through to your human heart, *miracles do happen!* Then nothing is held back; all is spent for the beloved. Abuse can no longer exist—not to the self, not to anyone. It is loving for the sake of loving alone.

too hurt to love

epilogue

I am deeply overwhelmed as I try to write the ending of this book. There is so much to say; so much to tell you about my family.

About my husband, Hank. At first my healing threw him off balance. He'd grown so used to walking the tightrope between Scott and me that when he didn't need to anymore he barely knew how to stand on level ground. He no longer needed to keep his iron guard up to protect Scott from me, or me from Scott. He could finally tell me how much it had hurt him to watch it, to feel it every single day. Now he could tell me how angry he was that I had rejected his son for so long. He could finally express his love for Scott openly and know I truly welcomed it with all my heart, that I looked for it, that I needed to see it to know, in some way, that Scott could still be fathered, as well as mothered—and that he could take in our love. Gradually, Hank and I began to trust each other's love for our children. There is no doubt today that we have birthed love for all three together.

When we first married and our battles were more frequent, Buff assumed that Scott had invaded her life too. Suddenly she had a little brother and could sense that even I had an issue with him. My rejection of Scott influenced her during those early years to reject him, in some ways, herself. But as she matured a bit, she attributed the contention between Scott and me to my "being in a bad mood," which was most of the time. Consequently, she dared not get too close to me either and began to feel compassion for Scott, since he was subject to my irritability on a daily basis. Today Buff and Scott share a mutual love and respect for each other in a close brother-sister relationship. Buff and her husband, Doug, have been married for nine years now. They carefully consider the raising of a child of their own, having both watched, firsthand, the evidences of the internal stress of an unequipped mother. This has significantly thwarted their enthusiasm to parent. Currently, Buff is in nursing school, which has placed this decision on hold for now.

And Kell has endured with us. She has watched me from a distance, but knows me well enough to sense any discrepancy between what I claim to be and who I am. She is keenly aware of any rejection from me. My misaligned relationship with Scott has confused her image of me and jeopardized her confidence in my ability to mother her. She has been tugged in the direction of loyalty to me on one hand, and disappointment in my ability to mother, on the other. On the same seesaw, she felt responsible for making up for my deficiencies with Scott, but frustrated with herself for being unable to make her own actions comply with her growing sympathy for him. Kell's hypersensitivity and keen ability to assimilate the effects of my dysfunction carry an incalculable price. She was married for eight years and is now divorced. She has no children.

"It's such a paradox to me," Kell says, "that as traumatic as life experiences are, we learn to improvise. Often this involves growing a thick skin to cover the thinner one, deteriorated by hate. Since Scottie, as a child, was surrounded by females who resented him, it seemed inevitable to me that he would grow up to hate women. As much as I felt sympathy for Scott and self-reproach for how I treated him, I couldn't accept that the opportunity to alleviate his hurt and answer his needs was within my realm of responsibility. Although I recognizd that my mother wasn't treating him right, my feeble attempts to make up for it were short-lived, and I became impatient and agitated again. I just could not seem to make my actions and attitude toward Scott comply with the way my heart felt he should be treated. It was very frustrating, and I was confused.

"I am grateful that perhaps all was not as irreparable as it appeared then. Both my mother and Scott are brilliant and discerning people. They have an esteem for each other that nobody else will ever quite understand. I believe their healing has occurred because they have each chosen to make their lives as functional as possible, that step by step they have developed love and respect for themselves and, in turn, for each other."

Scott, 24 and single, is keenly aware of his impaired childhood and his resulting vulnerabilities. In the wake of our miracle, Scott teetered emotionally, often withdrawing in confusion about his "new" mother. Fortunately, he has been willing to talk about his feelings and needs, both in retrospect and currently. These intimate sharing times have validated his experience. He tells me what it was like to be rejected and misunderstood. I invite him to tell me more and assure him it should never have been that way for him. Today the two of us share an affectionate and trusting love relationship that is priceless to me. Scott wanted to share his thoughts with you:

"Abuse is a disease that's as infectious as any drug addiction or blood-borne pathogen. What's important is to get help at each level—to stop the cycle before the trauma is passed on to the next generation. What my mother did for herself doesn't necessarily stop the sickness from spreading; the infection still resides within me. The only way to truly break the chain is for me to assume a portion of the responsibility of recovery by ceasing my own self-abuse and to begin to love myself before I ever consider having my own children and passing this plague on to them. As you can see, this book is in no way an ending; it is really just the beginning."

It is very difficult to describe the horrendous impact of one parent who cannot love his or her child. Although the parent herself is undoubtedly a victim of the generational transmission of such tragic losses and cannot birth the feeling of love, no matter how hard she tries, the consequences cannot be measured. There is no blame to be blamed. There is no excuse as a reason. There is only a desperate need for change. We must be able to provide a child with his own sense of self, a knowing of who he is, and courage to be that incredible person he was born to be. To let him know he can affect his world, that someone understands his unique and marvelous being. To care enough in ways that make sense to the child. To love in meaningful ways the child can understand.

It is no happenstance that I have become intricately involved in attachment relationships, especially between infant/child and caregiver. I now work as a therapist at Kennedy Krieger Institute, a Johns Hopkins facility in Baltimore, Maryland, serving families in facilitating the most profound relationship they will ever have.

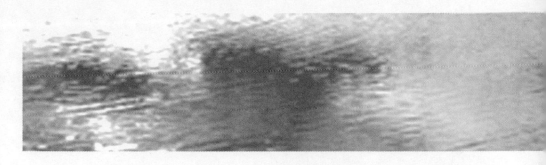

Sources of Help

Cindy Cook, M.S.W.
4550 Ten Oaks Road
Dayton, MD 21036
For information about workshops, therapy, or to be
placed on a mailing list for a newsletter, call 410-531-4815.

Breakthrough Workshops
Ann Smith Counseling & Training
4309 Linglestown Road, Suite 105-E
Harrisburg, PA 17112
717-545-7252

Caron Foundation
Galen Hall Road, Box A
Wernersville, PA 19565
215-678-5267

Haroldo E. Drachenberg, M.D., Psychiatrist
5550 Sterett Place
K & M Lakefront North Building, Suite 308
Columbia, MD 21044
410-997-8068

Kennedy Krieger Institute
Outpatient Psychiatry Center
1750 E. Fairmount Avenue, 4th Floor
Baltimore, MD 21231
410-502-8448; 410-502-9485

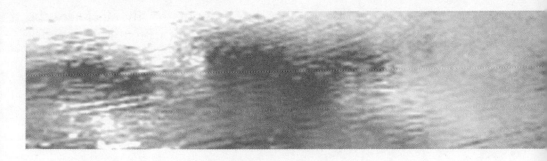

Assurances for the Wounded

I run my everyday thoughts through to God. It has become a habit now. Keeping Him so involved with me puts a holy spin on my every move. I love the divine camaraderie. My internal world is laced with Him; it's much like dipping ordinary metal into a tank of gold.

I want to share a few personal gems—thoughts, questions, insights—that I have retrieved from these intimate trysting times. They are to be read by the heart, slowly.

~ I must know it's OK with You if I love me.

~ Hold me in Your arms. Keep me sane. Hold Your love and my life in Your hands. Knead them together gently.

~ You absolutely adore me. I am the apple of Your eye, the center of Your attention.

~ You have plans for me—to prosper me and not to harm me. And I am equipped for them. These plans will make me happier than I could ever dream of being on my own. I am safe with You. Nothing can threaten or hurt me; nothing can diminish Your plan for me.

~ I want to go from grasping the hem of Your garment to sleeping like a baby in Your arms.

~ I want to feedback nurturing thoughts to myself. Make the part of me that abuses me, heal. I want to naturally care for me with unconditional love, as You do.

~ I'm OK, even if it doesn't work out.

~ I am what You made me to be, and that is someone very wonderful and precious.

~ I love who I am.

~ I can decide exactly how I want to be and whom I want to be in relationship with.

~ I can take incredible pride in my current situation if I follow Your plan.

~ It is Satan who wants me to abuse myself.

~ I am being cared for by You *in this very moment.*

~ I choose to release all extreme behaviors, beliefs, and emotions that keep me off balance.

~ You have made a way for Your untrusting children to trust You. I just want to put my head on Your shoulder and stay there for life.

~ To the degree that I take in Your love, I am not afraid.

~ From Your perspective, how big is my world?

~ You can love me any way You want. I know You will be gentle.

~ I can be my own ally and feel compassion for me, especially when I fail.

~ You want me to experience all the wonder of this life.

~ The brokenness is of the breaker, not of the Healer.

~ It's grace that makes everything all better.

~ I determine to trust Your mercy.

~ I am in trouble when I forget who I am.